Developmental Disabilities
and
Child Welfare

Ronald C. Hughes and Judith S. Rycus

CWLA Press • Washington, DC

CWLA Press is an imprint of the Child Welfare League of America.

The Child Welfare League of America (CWLA) is a privately supported, nonprofit, membership-based organization committed to preserving, protecting, and promoting the well-being of all children and their families. Believing that children are our most valuable resource, CWLA, through its membership, advocates for high standards, sound public policies, and quality services for children in need and their families.

CHILD WELFARE LEAGUE OF AMERICA, INC.
440 First Street, NW, Third Floor, Washington, DC 20001-2085
e-mail: books@cwla.org

CURRENT PRINTING (last digit)
10 9 8 7 6 5 4 3 2 1

Cover design by Jenny Geanakos
Text design by Cathy Corder

ISBN # 0-87868-734-3

Contents

UNDERSTANDING
DEVELOPMENTAL DISABILITIES

I t is likely that all of us have one or more developmental disorders. The processes of gestation and birth expose the fetus to many potentially hazardous complications. Thus, gestation and birth form an inexorable leveling mechanism. All of us have a touch of cerebral palsy and mental retardation, some more, some less—the pathological endowment of gestation and birth.

Most of us develop strategies to compensate for our developmental shortcomings. For most persons with poor eyesight, for example, a pair of eyeglasses adequately corrects the problem. A competent assistant likewise helps the absentminded executive to remember names and numbers and also corrects the boss's spelling. Similarly, the clumsy person develops ways to keep from bumping into and breaking things.

When, then, should we begin to view developmental problems as developmental disabilities? Degrees of dysfunction occur across a continuum that includes, at one end, a disorder that may be limited and merely a nuisance, and on the other end, a disorder that can be pervasive and potentially life-threatening. Determining where along this continuum a disorder would be severe enough to be termed a disability required functional definitions, rather than categorical ones.

The term "developmental disability" itself was first used by the federal government in the late 1970s in a move to expand the range of developmental disabilities that would make individuals eligible to receive federal funding and services. Previously, funding and services had been provided "categorically"; that is, only to persons with particular diagnosed conditions, generally mental retardation. The initial change in federal law was the expansion of eligible conditions to include cerebral palsy, epilepsy, and autism. However, this definition still excluded persons with other developmental problems who were equally in need of developmental and remedial services. Functional definitions eventually replaced the earlier categorical definitions and formulated criteria for eligibility based upon the effects of a developmental problem on the person's adaptive ability to function independently in a typical, age-appropriate life environment.

Functional definitions were adopted in federal legislation in 1978. This definition has been adapted and incorporated into most legislated definitions at the state level as well. In this definition, a developmental disability is a severe, chronic condition that

- Is caused by a mental or physical impairment, or a combination of such impairments;
- Shows signs of affecting the person before age 22;
- Is likely to last for a long time, perhaps a lifetime; and
- Makes it most difficult to do things in the following areas:
    - Self-care (to feed and dress and to take care of one's health);
    - Receptive and expressive language (to hear and understand what is being said and to be understood by others);
    - Learning (in both day-to-day and formal educational environments);
    - Mobility (to get around inside and outside of home, school, work, and community);
    - Self-direction (to make decisions about relationships with others and about jobs, education, money, and other important things);
    - Capacity for independent living (to live safely without assistance for at least half the time); and
    - Capacity for self-sufficiency (to work at a job and earn a living).

While this definition attempts to measure where developmental disability begins, the incorporation of such words and phrases as "severe," "chronic," "likely to," and "most likely" into the definition renders its interpretation somewhat ambiguous. This is not necessarily bad. Some ambiguity allows the professional diagnostician the latitude to weigh the variables given in this functional definition or to consider other variables in determining eligibility for services and support.

An important variable in this definition is the age of onset. Most definitions state that, to be considered developmental, the disability must manifest itself before a certain age. The upper limit in many definitions is age 22. In viewing human life as a continuing developmental process, however, any age limit appears arbitrary. Brain trauma causing epilepsy at age 17 may not appear significantly different from the same accident at age 23. Huntington's chorea, a progressive central nervous system disease that usually appears in the fifth decade of life, is a genetic disease—a developmental part of the individual's future, destined from conception. It is not considered a developmental disability, however, when its symptoms are first manifested later in life.

Still, there are significant reasons for recognizing an upper age limit of 18 to 21 years, other than fiscal or administrative utility. Although development continues throughout life, an important number of normal maturational milestones are typically attained by age 22 or earlier. Piaget suggests that formal operations, the most highly developed cognitive activities, are attained by late adolescence, if they are attained at all. Structural growth of the brain is completed by early adolescence, and most other physical maturation is completed by age 22. The emotional growth necessary for the achievement of a personal identity and a sense of an adequate and capable self, essential for adult activity, is typically formed by age 22, although modifications may take place throughout the life cycle. And by that time, most persons achieve a social maturity that allows them to accept and maintain a social role as a functional adult member of society.

The concentrated development that occurs during the first two decades of life, its maturational culmination, and the potentially pervasive destructive effects of disorders during this time can, in some respects, justify an upper age limit of 22. We will therefore use the following broad definition in our discussion of developmental disabilities and related child welfare issues:

A developmental disability is a condition or disorder, physical, cognitive, or emotional in nature, that has the potential to significantly interfere with the normal process of a child's growth and development. To be a developmental disability, the disorder must be present and affect the child before the age of 22.

Conditions and disorders that may be included in the category of developmental disabilities are mental retardation, cerebral palsy, epilepsy, autism, learning disabilities, speech and language disorders, spina bifida, hearing loss and deafness, visual disorders and blindness, orthopedic disorders, and congenital malformations. These developmental disabilities are often seen in children being served by the child welfare system. Many other developmental disabilities occur less frequently and are not discussed here.

Factors That Contribute to Developmental Disabilities

At times, it is possible to identify the specific factors that have caused a developmental disability. For example, children with Down's syndrome have an identifiable chromosome aberration. Epilepsy and cerebral palsy are, at times, caused by brain damage resulting from a severe blow to the head. However, the specific causes of most developmental disabilities cannot be determined with certainty, although many factors have been correlated with the presence of developmental disabilities. These factors may themselves cause the disability, or they may contribute to a sequence of events that ultimately results in a disability. The following section describes some of these contributing factors.

Genetic Inheritance

Our genes are the "blueprints" for our development. These genetic plans are transmitted through the reproductive cells of our parents and are present in every cell in our bodies. Disabilities that result from genetic governance are usually of three types: gene inheritance, chromosomal abnormality, and spontaneous mutations. Conditions such as phenylketonuria (PKU) and Tay-Sachs syndrome result from the inheritance of genes or combinations of genes that dictate the development of a disabling condition. Conditions such as Down's, Turner's, fragile-X, and Klinefelter's syndromes result from accidents in reproductive cell division that lead to abnormalities in chromosomes.

Although popularly believed to be a major cause of developmental disabilities, such genetic problems account for only a small percentage.

Many genetic abnormalities preclude fetal viability; the pregnancy often ends in miscarriage.

The contribution of genetics to disabling conditions is not, however, always clear. Some conditions are thought to be caused by a genetic predisposition combined with exposure to an "environmental trigger." If persons with a certain genetic makeup are exposed to some other condition—a virus, an environmental toxin, another illness, or trauma—they are more likely to develop the disabling condition. Without the trigger event, however, the genetically predisposed person does not develop the condition. Conversely, persons who lack the genetic predisposition will not develop the condition, even with exposure to the trigger.

Trauma

Traumatic injury to a child through a direct blow or assault can cause severe disability. Such an injury is especially dangerous when the brain or central nervous system is affected. The area of the brain that is injured and the extent of the brain damage together determine the nature and severity of the resulting disability.

Auto accidents and falls onto hard surfaces such as concrete are common causes of head injury in children. Child abuse is also a frequent cause of head and central nervous system injury in infants and young children, as is "shaken baby syndrome." Mental retardation, cerebral palsy, and epilepsy are some of the possible outcomes of child abuse, including shaking an infant or young child.

Exposure to Toxic Substances

The ingestion of toxic chemicals and substances by a pregnant woman can seriously interfere with normal fetal growth and development. Alcohol, tobacco, some prescription medications, street drugs, and fumes from materials such as paint, glue, and varnish are all toxic substances that can be harmful to the fetus. Exposure to radiation, such as X-rays, is also in this category. Ingestion of poisonous substances by children may also result in developmental disabilities.

Fetal alcohol syndrome (FAS) is a common disability in infants of women who consume large amounts of alcohol while pregnant. Alcohol destroys and damages cells in the central nervous system, and widespread destruction of brain cells in early fetal development results in malformations in the developing brain structures. Fetal alcohol syndrome includes both prenatal and postnatal growth deficiency, mental retardation, microcephaly, behavior disorders, and problems in motor control. Fetal alcohol effects (FAE), a less serious form of the disorder, can occur when a mother consumes a moderate amount of alcohol during pregnancy.

Prenatal exposure to crack cocaine and other drugs can also have a destructive effect on fetal development. Low birth weight, growth retardation, a high rate of perinatal complications, and neurological problems are all associated with crack cocaine abuse.

Maternal Age and Health

A higher risk of developmental disabilities may be associated with a maternal age below 15 or over 35. Poor health of the mother during pregnancy is also associated with disabilities in the fetus. Chronic illnesses, such as diabetes, high blood pressure, severe anemia, hypothyroidism, kidney disease, and congenital heart disease can negatively affect fetal development, but are much less likely to have adverse effects if well-monitored and treated during the pregnancy. Extreme obesity of the mother has also been associated with disabilities. Malnutrition of the mother before and/or during the pregnancy increases risk of disability in newborns.

Complications During Pregnancy and Birth

At one time, Rh-incompatibility was a major cause of infant morbidity. The Rh factor refers to the presence or absence of a particular substance in the blood (hence, Rh+ or Rh-). Rh incompatibility occurs when a mother with an Rh- factor carries a fetus with an Rh+ factor. With this condition, the mother's immune system develops antibodies that attack and destroy the red blood cells of the fetus. This can cause brain damage in the developing fetus. A first child usually is not seriously affected. The first pregnancy sensitizes the mother's immune system, which results in increased problems in subsequent pregnancies and a higher risk of brain damage in later-born children. A special injection therapy successfully desensitizes the mother's immune system, allowing the fetus to develop normally. Prenatal identification of the Rh incompatibility and proper medical treatment are critical to prevent brain damage in the infant.

Complications during labor and delivery, such as prolonged and difficult labor, premature separation of the placenta, or a knotted or prolapsed umbilical cord, can cause brain and central nervous system damage from anoxia, or deprivation of oxygen to the brain. A high percentage of infants born with cerebral palsy are thought to have sustained birth injury.

Improper use of forceps during delivery can sometimes result in brain damage from direct trauma. Overuse of anesthesia for the mother may lead to asphyxia in the newborn. Careful fetal monitoring, the use of cesarean section delivery during high-risk childbirth, and sophisticated infant intensive care units have reduced the occurrence of birth-related injury and disability.

Minimizing complications of pregnancy and birth, however, depends upon access to and use of appropriate health care. Many children and families served by the child welfare system do not have access to proper health care or do not utilize available services.

Prematurity

Neither the premature infant nor its mother is prepared for the birth process, and the infant is not fully developed for survival in the postnatal environment. These factors increase the risk of developmental disabilities. Contractions that push the undeveloped child against an undilated and uneffaced cervix can cause central nervous system damage. The lungs of a premature infant may not be sufficiently developed to allow normal breathing. An excess of oxygen, such as may be found in poorly controlled isolettes and incubators, has been associated with infant blindness and brain damage.

Viral and Bacterial Infections

Rubella, or German measles, is a common and relatively mild viral infection. Symptoms are flu-like and generally last only a few days. If a pregnant mother contracts rubella, however, there are significant risks to the fetus, particularly during the first trimester of pregnancy when the fetus's brain and vital organs are developing. Rubella can cause blindness, deafness, congenital heart defects, and mental retardation. A high percentage of children who are both blind and deaf were exposed to rubella early in pregnancy. Immunization therapy has made it possible to eliminate rubella as a cause of developmental disabilities. Yet, there are still children being born whose mothers have not been properly immunized.

Several venereal diseases are associated with developmental disabilities. Syphilis, a bacterial disease, attacks and destroys brain and central nervous system tissue in its later stages. It is usually responsive to antibiotic therapy; however, if undetected or left untreated in an infected mother, it presents a risk of brain damage to the fetus. Gonorrhea, another bacterial disease, can lead to infant blindness when present in the birth canal during childbirth. Routine application of antibiotics to infants' eyes immediately after birth is a precautionary measure against gonorrhea. Unfortunately, in recent years, strains of both syphilis and gonorrhea have become resistant to previously effective antibiotic therapy.

Variations of the herpes virus are common infective agents in humans. Chicken pox and shingles are caused by a herpes virus. Another variation of the virus, herpes simplex I, is the common cause of cold sores of the mouth and may occasionally be associated with genital lesions. The common cause of herpes-related venereal disease is herpes simplex II. This disease typically causes recurring painful blisters and sores in and around the genitals, anus, or mouth. If active sores are present in the genital area during childbirth, the infant may contract the virus from the mother. Infection of the infant may lead to severe neurological damage or death. Developmental problems may be avoided through cesarean section delivery when active herpes is present.

Meningitis, encephalitis, and other viral and bacterial illnesses can directly affect the central nervous system and are associated with subsequent brain damage. Excessively high fever associated with severe viral or bacterial infections is also at times associated with brain damage. The human immunodeficiency virus (HIV) can also be transmitted from pregnant women to their babies.

Toxoplasmosis, a parasitic organism that may be found in cat litter boxes, has been associated with central nervous system damage and mental retardation. Pregnant women should avoid contact with cat feces.

Nutrition

Numerous research studies have demonstrated the negative effects of poor nutrition on children's growth and development. The prenatal period and the first two years of life are characterized by extensive and rapid brain and central nervous system growth. Good nutrition is required during these periods to promote healthy cell development. Malnutrition of the mother during pregnancy, and of the young child, can interfere with healthy development. Malnutrition is thought to be a probable contributor in many milder cases of mental retardation.

Exposure of a fetus or an infant to deleterious prenatal, perinatal, and postnatal factors will not always result in a disability. Mediating variables include the amount of exposure to the contributing condition (large amounts of exposure and extended exposures constitute higher risk); the genetic and constitutional predispositions of the mother and the fetus; and the age of the fetus or child when the exposure takes place. (Some exposures are more likely to cause problems during the first trimester of pregnancy, when the fetus's vital organ systems are developing; on the other hand, younger children are more likely to recover from serious neurological trauma than are older children.) It can be concluded, however, that infants who have been exposed to any of the contributing factors will have a higher risk of developing disabilities than children who have not been so exposed. Many of the factors that may contribute to disabling conditions can be avoided or prevented through education and preventive health care.

Child Abuse and Neglect and Developmental Disabilities

There is considerable evidence to suggest a significant interrelationship between child abuse and neglect and developmental disabilities. Many factors that are common in situations of abuse and neglect are also common correlates of developmental disabilities: poor diet and nutrition; lack of regular and adequate medical care, including poor prenatal care; an unsanitary and unhealthy environment, with higher risk of exposure to harmful and toxic substances; high incidence of drug and alcohol abuse; poor supervision of children and resultant higher risk of injury; and lack of nurturing and stimulation. It appears that developmental disability is both a cause and an effect of child abuse and neglect.

Many studies have suggested a direct link between physical abuse and developmental disability or delay. Studies of physically abused children have documented significant neuromotor handicaps, including central nervous system damage, physical defects, growth and mental retardation, and serious speech problems. Cognitive and language deficits have also been noted in abused children [National Research Council 1993]. A study of 42 abused children by Martin [1972] conducted over a three-year period found the following:

- Forty-three percent of the study group had a neurological abnormality on follow-up examination. Martin concludes that "permanent damage to the brain is a frequent sequela of physical abuse."

- Thirty-three percent of the study group were functioning at a retarded level, with a measured I.Q. of less than 80. Martin states, "It is clear that there is an intimate relationship between central nervous system insult and residual retardation."

- A large number of the abused children demonstrated "absent, minimal or impaired speech and language." Martin notes that 75% of the children with language delays were of normal intelligence. It can be inferred that abuse interfered with the acquisition and use of language in children.

Environmental factors common in neglectful situations are thought to contribute to developmental problems. Martin refers to the work of Harlow and Spitz, Provence, and Lipton, among others, who report that environmental deprivation, such as that experienced by institutionalized infants, can result in retardation. Martin also stresses the role of undernutrition in subsequent developmental delay. In an earlier study, Chase and Martin [1970] concluded that permanent retardation can result from undernutrition in the first year of life. Helfer et al. [1976] assert, "The most disturbing and consistent finding in observation of young children who have been abused and neglected is the delay, or arrest, of their development." These authors have noted a variety of developmental problems in abused and neglected children, including difficulty in feeding; delay in motor development with poor muscle tone; delay in social development and social responses, such as smiling and vocalization; a lack of activity; a generalized apathy toward objects and people; a consistent and considerable delay in speech; and the absence of reaction when separated from parents. Problematic school performance, such as low grades, poor test scores, and frequent grade retention, is a fairly consistent finding in studies of physically abused and neglected children, with neglected children appearing the most adversely affected [National Research Council 1993].

A developmentally disabled child is also at a high risk of being abused or neglected. Steele [1987] refers to the three major criteria found to be highly correlated with child abuse:

- The parents must have the potential to abuse; a particular set of personal parent factors predisposes a parent to be abusive.

- The child is viewed by the parent as somehow special; the child who is different, who requires special care, or who is perceived as unlike other children is at potentially higher risk of abuse.

- A crisis, or series of crises, including high stress and accompanying inability to cope, tends to precipitate the abuse.

Children with disabilities may indeed be different from other children or may be perceived as different by their parents. They may differ in physical appearance or capacity; they may require specialized care and treatment; they may not be able to respond socially or emotionally to the parents' expectations. Parents of developmentally disabled children frequently mourn the loss of a "normal" child. Anger is part of the mourning process, and it can sometimes be turned outward by abusive parents toward the disabled child. Additionally, the presence of a disabled chid creates numerous emotional and environmental stresses for the family, and the resulting emotional turmoil can reach crisis proportions. Therefore, if parents have the psychological potential to abuse, a disabled child is often at higher risk of abuse than are other children.

Children with disabilities may also be subject to a special type of neglect. The child's exceptional needs for care and treatment may create a situation of neglect through no fault of the parents. A family that can manage adequately under normal circumstances may not have the personal or financial resources to meet the exceptional medical, nutritional, social, and educational needs of a child with a disabilities, thereby creating a situation of inadequate and insufficient care of the child.

The strong correlation between abuse or neglect and developmental disabilities is further illustrated by the numbers of children with disabilities who are served by the public child welfare system. A study completed by the Ohio Department of Human Services reported that approximately 20% of all children in out-of-home care were mentally retarded or developmentally disabled [Institute For Child Advocacy 1987]. Another study, conducted in Hennepin County, Minnesota, suggested that 40% of all children receiving services from child welfare agencies had developmental problems [Richardson et al. 1989].

Barriers to Effective Services

The escalating numbers of abused and neglected children and the potentiating relationship between child maltreatment and developmental disabilities support the need for an approach to serving children that actively considers both areas. Yet in spite of this, public social service systems continue to provide categorical or separate services for child maltreatment and for developmental disabilities. Many factors contribute to this problem, including a serious lack of coordination between community social agencies that serve children with developmental disabilities and their families [Richardson et al. 1989] and a widespread lack of knowledge and skill regarding disabilities among professional staff in most social service systems [Martin & Laidlow 1980; Falconer 1982].

Child welfare services and services to children with developmental disabilities are frequently separated at the federal, state, and local levels. These services are funded from different sources, administered by different bodies, and delivered by separate local agencies. Service delivery objectives often appear to be quite different, each focusing on the remediation of different conditions and defined by a perception of quite different presenting problems. And, while services are available, they remain inaccessible due in large part to barriers erected out of philosophical and legislative differences among agencies and programs. A survey by Richardson and associates also suggested that ignorance on the part of staff members in one agency about how to access or use services in another agency created barriers to the accessibility of services for children with developmental disabilities [Richardson et al. 1989].

A review of the literature suggests that a lack of training of child welfare workers is a common contributor to poor services provided to children with developmental disabilities. Kurtz [1979] strongly suggests that a lack of knowledge and skill in child welfare workers is a serious impediment to the identification of children with disabilities and to the provision of early intervention services. Kurtz believes that many child welfare workers have a general understanding of child development but lack sufficient knowledge and skill related to disabilities. Therefore, they do not recognize or cannot make accurate judgments about early signs of disabling conditions. He suggests that lack of training may explain why children with disabilities are often underrepresented in child welfare statistics.

Schilling et al. [1986] concur that the child protection system may not recognize and document children in the child welfare system who have disabilities. The authors claim that the lack of training is a significant contributor, as "few social workers, even those with graduate degrees, have had developmental disabilities courses" and cannot assess these conditions, particularly when they are mild in nature. Finally, Coyne and Brown [1985; 1986] suggest that caseworkers' lack of accurate information about developmental disabilities interferes with proper placement of children with disabilities in adoptive families.

Summary

The child welfare field is evolving toward a developmental, family-centered orientation to services that is concerned with prevention, as well as remedy. Therefore, we must develop our system's ability to identify maltreated children who have, or are at risk of, developmental disabilities. Their needs must be properly assessed, and early coordinated and integrated services must be provided. (The child welfare caseworker will often assume a case management and advocacy role in assuring that these children and their families receive comprehensive specialized services.)

The following chapters review the conditions most commonly seen by child welfare workers, describe specific signs and symptoms of these conditions, and describe the most appropriate interventions. These chapters were designed to assist child welfare professionals in their efforts to become more knowledgeable about developmental disabilities and to emphasize the central role that the child welfare field plays in serving children with developmental disabilities and their families.

MYTHS AND MISCONCEPTIONS ABOUT DEVELOPMENTAL DISABILITIES

Myths and misconceptions regarding developmental disabilities have been prevalent in most cultures, and persons with disabilities have commonly been viewed with fear, suspicion, and pity. These attitudes and misconceptions are reflected in our language. The word "handicap" is an epithet derived from the practice of holding cap in hand, i.e., begging [Handicapism 1976]. Begging was institutionalized by English law and was a regulated entitlement of the disabled.

The word "seizure," which refers to the random spasmodic motor activity associated with some epilepsies, was born of the belief that affected persons were "seized" or possessed by the devil. Children born deformed or disabled were called changelings; it was believed that, before birth, they had been changed or substituted by the devil for the normal children of God. Midwives attending such births, or priests who had blessed the pregnant mothers, were often suspect. These unfortunate persons sometimes lost their lives because of their suspected collusion with the devil. Such "children of the devil" were often allowed to die, or were even put to death within an obligatory ethic. Infanticide for children with developmental disabilities has been sanctioned in many cultures throughout history [Rosen et al. 1976].

Today, science enlightens us. The etiologies of developmental disabilities are no longer considered diabolical. What was once righteous intercession has become benign neglect in hospital delivery rooms, with the same results: misinformed decisions are made to allow children with developmental disabilities to die at birth. Some persons with disabilities still beg, and most people still expect this and respond with pity. Persons with grand mal epilepsy are still often viewed as possessed by something foreign and beyond their control, in spite of the fact that approximately half are seizure-free with medication, and seizures are significantly reduced for many others. We may have forgotten the roots of the words we use to label and describe people with disabilities, and the harmful stereotypic and prejudicial attitudes have become less blatant and more subtle—but they are equally entrenched. The words no longer scream their prejudice, but instead, propound subtly, not arousing us to reflect.

Child welfare professionals will regularly encounter negative stereotypes, attitudes, and misconceptions in the community; in some families of children with disabilities; among professional groups, including physicians, educators, and social workers; and probably within themselves. Such attitudes can seriously interfere with case management, and the adequate delivery of services to persons with disabilities and their families. It is the purpose of this section to help workers to become aware of these attitudes and misconceptions, and to develop an awareness of our own misconceptions and harmful stereotypic attitudes.

Myth #1

Developmental disabilities are clearly defined, visible conditions that are permanent and constant disabling factors in a child's life, and will therefore prevent active involvement in much of life's normal activities.

The term developmental disability is not easily defined, and, since its inception, has included a changing variety of conditions. Federal legislation originally designated four conditions as developmental disabilities: epilepsy, autism, cerebral palsy, and mental retardation. More recent federal law does not refer to particular conditions, but rather to the effects of any condition on growth and adaptation.

All disabling conditions have the potential to interfere with, retard, or alter the course of a child's physical, cognitive, social, and emotional development, but the degree and nature of such effects depend upon a number of social and environmental factors.

Developmental disabilities are varied and complicated phenomena, and the degree to which a condition presents adaptive problems is different for different persons. Two factors can influence the degree to which any condition will be disabling: the extent and severity of the condition, and the availability of corrective, supportive, or rehabilitative help.

Most disabling conditions can range in severity from very mild to very severe. The greater the severity of a condition, the greater the potential for interference with a child's growth and development. However, once the means and technology are available to remedy or correct a condition so that it no longer significantly interferes with adaptation, the condition ceases to be disabling. Prior to the invention of corrective lenses, vision problems could significantly interfere with daily living. Anyone who is severely nearsighted can attest to the pervasive problems he or she would have in mobility, employment, and general survival without eyeglasses.

Many other potentially disabling conditions have become correctable or made less debilitating through advances in science and technology. Congenital heart problems can be remedied by corrective surgery; braces and other orthopedic apparatuses enable many children with spina bifida and cerebral palsy to sit, stand, or walk; motorized wheelchairs, specially equipped vans, ramps, and wheelchair-accessible curbs allow independent mobility and transportation; anticonvulsant medication can prevent or significantly reduce the incidence of epileptic seizures; and sign language provides a complete, rich means of communication for persons who are hearing impaired. As technology develops, and science unravels the mysteries of many disabilities, one may expect fewer and fewer conditions to be disabling. Brain pacemakers to regulate neural impulses, bionic replacement of limbs, drugs to correct biochemical and enzyme imbalances, and computerized boxes that talk at the push of a button are some of the new technological advances that could revolutionize our thinking about disabilities.

Supportive interventions can also help minimize the effects of a condition on adaptive functioning. For example, a personal assistant, who provides assistance with dressing, feeding, bathing, laundry, meal preparation, transportation, cognitive and life management activities, and/or infant and child care can facilitate a person with a disabling condition to participate fully in work, community, and social environments.

Early Intervention

A child's development is a dynamic process. The general nature of development is determined in large part by genes. A common heredity predisposes most children to perform various developmental tasks in an

order and time frame similar to other children, as part of typical maturation. The particular outcomes of development for any child, however,
will be ultimately determined by the child's interaction with the environment, and the child's success or failure in mastering the challenges presented by social and environmental pressures.

The process of development is cumulative. Early successes in mastering age-appropriate tasks build a foundation for mastering later, more
complex skills. Conversely, failure to master early tasks can interfere with
later development. When a disabling condition prevents a child from becoming involved in the activities and experiences that stimulate normal
growth, the child's development may be delayed and perhaps altered, and
the negative effects of the disability may be compounded over time. Physical, social, cognitive, and emotional development all affect and are affected by each other. An undiagnosed or untreated disability in one area
can have negative effects on other areas as well.

Early recognition of disabilities, and timely remedial and supportive
services are essential to maximize a child's potential for more healthy
growth and development. Early intervention can often correct or help
compensate for disabling conditions, prevent the cumulative negative effects of the condition on normal growth, and guard against deterioration.
Even for children whose disabilities are so severe that they cannot be
expected to exhibit typical development with even the most timely and
appropriate intervention, early recognition and intervention can help prevent deterioration, and enhance continuing adaptation.

Myth #2

*Developmental disabilities are unfortunate accidents of nature,
and there is little that can be done to avoid or prevent them.*

The discussion in Chapter 1 of causal and contributing factors to
disabilities illustrated that many of these factors are environmentally determined, and therefore, may be modifiable. A knowledge of these factors, and a commitment to providing a safe and healthy environment for
a developing child can often prevent disabilities. Prevention includes, for
example, avoiding drug and alcohol use during pregnancy; rearing children in environments free of abuse or neglect; accessing timely prenatal

care; assuring adequate nutrition of pregnant women and young children; avoiding toxic fumes and substances; treating maternal health conditions; vaccinating all children against diseases; and others.

The concept of prevention cannot be limited, however, to the prevention of the occurrence of a disabling condition. Despite our best efforts, some children will continue to be born with or will develop disabling conditions. The concept of prevention must also include limiting the negative effects of a condition, and preventing subsequent physical, social, cognitive, and emotional deterioration.

Leland and Smith [1974] discuss three additional important aspects of prevention:

- *Preventing the growth or extension of a condition.* When disabling conditions do occur, further exacerbation of the condition can often be avoided. For example, the timely insertion of a shunt can arrest progressive brain damage from hydrocephalus, and careful dietary control will prevent the mental retardation associated with untreated phenylketonuria. (Phenylketonuria, or PKU, is a metabolic disorder in which the child lacks an enzyme to break down a protein commonly found in most foods. The toxic accumulation of this protein causes progressive brain damage and retardation. Avoidance of this protein in food while the brain is growing can prevent retardation, even though the child will always have PKU.)

- *Prevention of negative social effects.* Negative stereotypes, misconceptions, and prejudices can compound the social problems experienced by persons with disabilities. With proper education, individuals, families, and professionals can become more aware of the negative effects such attitudes can have on the social adjustment of persons with disabilities. Such awareness also promotes a more realistic assessment of the disability and appropriate professional intervention.

- *Prevention of later deterioration.* An individual who is limited in adaptive skills or who lacks resources will generally have more difficulty managing life tasks. The consequences may be a deterioration in all areas of the individual's functioning. A variety of readily available supportive and developmental services for persons with disabilities can enhance the development of adaptive skills, contribute to coping resources, and thereby prevent deterioration in functioning.

Myth #3

Developmentally disabled children have very different service needs than other children. Services to these children must be provided by personnel highly trained in work with the developmentally disabled if they are to effectively meet the disabled child's needs.

Viewing a child with a developmental disability as distinctly different from other children is misleading. A focus on specific presenting problems fosters this misconception. Most specialized children's services are remedial in nature, designed to confront and resolve any one of a number of conditions and problems. For example, children might be denoted as abused, neglected, developmentally disabled, physically ill, economically deprived, or needing special education. Services are then developed to address the particular presenting problem.

Specialized fields of practice ensure that difficult problems can be addressed with a depth of knowledge and expertise not often found in a generic setting. However, an awareness of the child's other basic needs, and the interrelationships among all areas of the child's development, is often missing in this categorical approach to services. Disabilities, for example, often become the focus of attention, and their significance is exaggerated; or the importance of other factors in the child's life, including those shared with typical children, are discounted. A case example illustrates this point. It was presented by a foster care caseworker in a workshop on developmental disabilities.

Case Example: Sally

Sally was a five-year-old child with severe cerebral palsy and an undetermined degree of mental retardation. She had been in several foster homes since being permanently surrendered by her biological mother at age two. Her most recent foster family had moved out of state, and because of limited foster home resources, the agency resorted to placing Sally in a nursing home facility until a more appropriate placement could be found.

Jean A, age 23, met Sally while doing volunteer work at the nursing home during her last year of college. After graduating, Ms. A was employed as a nurse's aide in a hospital, and she hoped to return to school to pursue an advanced degree in nursing. She had been assigned to work with Sally during her field experience, and afterwards she continued to visit Sally several times a week. She brought Sally toys and books, talked to her, fed her, sang to her, and developed an affection for and commitment to the child. After more than a year, she asked to adopt Sally.

The foster care worker was at a loss. She had limited experience with children with developmental disabilities, and even less experience with their adoption. She brought the case up for discussion during the workshop, in hopes that the trainer could tell her how to proceed.

The group discussion focused on the basic principles of adoption practice. The group considered Ms. A's level of personal maturity despite her youth; the degree of her demonstrated commitment to Sally; her experience with and ability to tolerate stress; her expectations for the child over time; her own emotional support systems—friends and family—since she would be a single parent; her ability to support herself and a child; her plan for the care of Sally while she was in school; and her willingness to undergo the changes in her life that would result from the responsibility of caring for a young child.

Sally's needs were also discussed: the agency's preference for a permanent home for her rather than foster or nursing home care; evidence that a close relationship had developed between Sally and Ms. A; and how to plan and effect a move that would be the least traumatic for Sally. Increased visiting, including visits to Ms. A's home, and thorough planning by Ms. A in preparation for bringing Sally home, would have to be encouraged before approving the adoption plan.

Much of the case discussion took place without reference to Sally's disabling condition, since it was not relevant. Because Sally had the universal needs of all children, her adoption was viewed from the perspective of all older-child adoptions. The disability was an important factor, but only to document Ms. A's ability to provide the special medical care and rehabilitative services Sally needed. Her nursing background and an available adoption subsidy quickly resolved these issues in her favor. The worker became more comfortable with her role when she realized that Sally's disability did not change the fundamentals of adoption planning.

Most children with disabilities are more similar than dissimilar to other children, and trained child welfare workers can generally be effective in providing case management services to them. Special services pertinent to the disability can be provided by specialized service systems in much the same way as services are provided to meet the special needs of any child. Training workers in competencies from other service systems, such as mental retardation and developmental disabilities, and in skills for interagency collaboration greatly increases the effectiveness of child welfare casework and case management activities for children with special needs.

Myth #4

Children with disabilities can be helped best to learn and grow in specialized settings where they can be with children similar to themselves. They should not have to compete with children who do not have disabilities, nor be exposed to the cruel remarks of such children.

This belief often reflects a well-meaning attempt to serve the best interests of children with disabilities. Proponents feel that specialized programs ensure that the children's special needs are better met, and that they are protected from feelings of inadequacy and inferiority. In practice, however, this attitude can reinforce segregation, promote stereotyping and prejudice, and may even deny many children a place as contributing members of society.

Segregationist attitudes can be institutionalized through such programs and activities as special recreation programs for persons with mental retardation, or "the handicapped children's day at the zoo." These programs and practices draw attention to children with disabilities as a group who are identified primarily by their common developmental conditions— a group more similar to each other than to children without disabilities. Children with disabilities are thus perceived as so different that we must educate and entertain them in their own separate group, guarding and protecting them from the larger society. There is also an implicit assumption that children with disabilities cannot function in the larger society.

Special programming may, at times, be valuable and beneficial for children with developmental disabilities. In some respects, IEPs (Individual Education Plans) and IFSPs (Individual Family Service Plans) formalize the development of special interventions that directly address a child's and his or her family's unique needs. However, if special programs are intended to replace integrated programs, there are significant liabilities for children both with and without disabilities.

Segregation may interfere with the healthy growth and development of children with disabilities. Throughout childhood, considerable learning takes place through identification and modeling of the behaviors of other children. When a child is deprived of routine involvement with typical children, his or her environment is an inaccurate representation of social reality. The child who is raised in segregated environments is denied the opportunity to explore, experience, and learn in the larger social environment. He or she may be sentenced to a life of overprotection and segregation; or, if expected to enter society as a productive adult, will be at a serious disadvantage.

Healthy and optimal growth for any child is best facilitated in a healthy and typical environment that provides for both general and exceptional needs, but which does not place the child outside of everyday social realities. Any program that segregates its recipients has an inherently negative effect on the population it is attempting to serve. The logistic requirements for, and benefits of, such a program must clearly and substantially outweigh its negative aspects before it can be considered valid.

Segregation of persons with disabilities is also a disservice to society, as it promotes and perpetuates stereotyping, misconceptions, and prejudice. Segregation denies most people day-to-day exposure to persons with disabilities, and there is no opportunity for myth to be replaced by fact learned from direct experience. Additionally, without interpersonal contact in typical everyday environments, society may not recognize the individual differences and competencies among persons with disabilities, and may not benefit from their potential contributions.

An extension of this myth is that people with disabilities prefer life and activities with "their own kind." It is true that years of segregation can contribute to feelings of anxiety and fear when a person with a disability is confronted with an integrated environment. When he or she withdraws to the safety of a more familiar environment, it is then interpreted as the cause and justification for segregation practices, rather than their effect. This myth is often a rationalization to cover and reinforce our own discomfort in the presence of persons with disabilities.

Children who are reared in everyday interaction with disabled children relate to the disability as a matter of course; the disability becomes a single, and not always relevant, characteristic in understanding the nature of the person.

Myth #5

Many children with disabilities need special services if they are to grow and develop to their fullest potential, and often these can be best provided in special settings: treatment facilities, group homes, and schools.

It is not our intent to deny the necessity for, or the effectiveness of, specialized services. The problem is not with the existence of these services when used judiciously, but rather with assigning an individual to special or segregated services that far exceed their domain of efficacy, thus depriving people with disabilities of integrated services when they are adequate and appropriate. This can be illustrated by the concept of educational mainstreaming, or inclusion. Inclusion should not be interpreted as "dumping" all children, regardless of need or condition, into a regular public classroom setting without appropriate support.

The primary federal legislation affecting the education of children with disabilities is P.L. 94-142, the Education of All Handicapped Children Act, which was passed in 1975. The legislation was amended in 1986, and again in 1990-91, and is now known as the Individuals with Disabilities Education Act (IDEA). This legislation stresses the importance of early intervention and individualized educational planning for children in the least restrictive environment. This means that child who can learn in a regular classroom should not be in a special class. A child who needs individualized attention and can receive it in a regular classroom with individualized instruction, or in a special education group in a public school, should not attend a segregated school. And finally, a child who can learn and grow in a specially structured school program should not be limited to a home tutor. The least restrictive environment is the most integrated social and educational environment in which the child can function. For example, it may not be appropriate to insist that an adolescent with cerebral palsy or other orthopedic conditions, and who has normal intelligence but must use a wheelchair, be sent to a special school. With ramps and elevators, a tape recorder, and perhaps occasional note-taking assistance from other students, (all referred to as "reasonable accommodation"), the regular high school classroom may well be managed, and offers a more normal adolescent educational and social experience.

Individualized health, educational, and social services are essential components of a total approach to growth and development for children with disabilities. However, when assignment to special programs is not clearly determined to be the best possible approach based upon the child's needs, it must be viewed as segregationist, limiting, and damaging to the child's potential development. The fact is, what the child misses in socialization, communication, and education from the integrated environment usually far exceeds the potential benefits of the specialized attention presumed available only in the special environment.

Myth #6

Persons with developmental disabilities are . . .

Any number of descriptive words or phrases could complete this potentially misleading statement. Although certain descriptive characteristics might provide some information about certain people, persons with developmental disabilities are not a homogeneous group. Disabling conditions vary widely; even the nature, severity, and effects of a particular disabling condition may be different for different persons.

Persons with developmental disabilities are unique individuals whose needs, skills, strengths, and personal traits span the continuum of possible human characteristics. The fact that many individuals may have the same disabling condition does not make them any more alike than does having other traits in common, such as short stature, blue eyes, or a hobby of stamp collecting. Yet the myths surrounding developmental disabilities include many stereotyped images.

Stereotyping usually results from misinformation. For example, it is commonly believed that people with epilepsy have no control over their seizures. This belief persists in spite of the fact that anticonvulsant medication renders nearly 50% seizure free, and helps another 30% significantly.

Stereotyping may also result from overgeneralizing basically valid information. For example, it is true that people with cerebral palsy may also be mentally retarded. But it is also true that people with cerebral palsy are often intellectually typical of the general population. Persons who have cerebral palsy and mental retardation have two disabilities, involving different areas of the brain. The disabilities might both have resulted from the same insult or trauma; however, the presence of one condition in no way assures the presence of the other.

Stereotypes regarding persons who are mentally retarded are particularly misleading. Some common beliefs are that they are generally ignorant, socially inept, and usually incapable of responsible action and self-support. The truth is quite different. Mental retardation ranges from mild to profound. Eighty to ninety percent of all persons with mental retardation fall within the mild category, and are variously capable in decision making, responsible action, social understanding, and self-sufficiency.

Stereotypes exist regarding families that have children with developmental disabilities. Consider the following:

• Most families of children with disabilities resent the special needs of the child, and are often happier if their children are placed in substitute care.

• Parents of children with disabilities are strong people who will do anything to ensure their child has the best possible care, and are committed to keeping the child at home if at all possible.

Both views are polarizations on a continuum of possible responses. Families fitting both descriptions exist, but families of children with disabilities do not have a special style, or configuration of personalities, or responses to their children. Regardless of what valid general information we possess regarding developmental disabilities, each case must be assessed individually and objectively.

When working with families of children with disabilities, we must be consistently aware of the potentially harmful effects of stereotyping. While we often use generalized information to help us better understand a particular condition, we should never apply any assumption drawn from general information to an individual child, without first assessing its validity for that child. Individualized assessment and treatment planning are as critical for children with disabilities, and their families, as in all other aspects of child welfare practice.

Myth #7

Diagnostic labels are always useful tools in assessing and understanding an individual's developmental disability.

Diagnostic labels are, very simply, tools that can facilitate precise and concise communication. But any tool may be inadequate, or the person using it may not understand its proper use. The overinclusive nature of some labels limits their diagnostic utility. For example, the label mental retardation, even with subcategories of mild, moderate, severe, and profound, does not sufficiently differentiate the subtleties found in intellectual capability and adaptive functioning of persons with mental retardation. In another example, a label of pervasive developmental disorder, autism, or childhood schizophrenia may be given to similar presenting symptoms. We may assume different etiologies, and plan different treatment strategies based upon which label is assigned, yet the only significant factor for a differential diagnosis may be the age of onset.

One must be alert to the possibilities of misdiagnosis or misuse of a label. Child welfare professionals should have a basic understanding of diagnostic principles and categories. Good case management includes knowing the credentials and abilities of the professionals who are sought for diagnostic consultation.

Negative expectations that are often derived from a diagnostic label can become self-fulfilling. A research study has demonstrated, for example, that when children were arbitrarily labeled "academic spurters," classroom teachers developed high expectations for them, and they progressed better than children not so labeled, even when there were no significant differences between the groups. [Rosenthal & Jacobson 1968]. Labels that connote negative expectations similarly can have a negative effect on the ensuing behavior of the persons so labeled.

While diagnostic labels are useful tools of communication, professionals must be constantly aware of the potentially harmful effects that can result from misunderstanding and misusing them.

CEREBRAL PALSY

C erebral palsy refers to a group of conditions where damage to the brain causes problems in movement and motor functioning. According to the United Cerebral Palsy Research and Educational Foundation, cerebral palsy may be defined as

> ... a group of conditions, usually originating in childhood, characterized by paralysis, weakness, incoordination, or any other aberration of motor function caused by pathology of the motor control center of the brain [Thain et al. 1980].

There are multiple potential causes of cerebral palsy, including prenatal and postnatal abuse and neglect. Most often, cerebral palsy is present at birth and is thought to be the result of some prenatal insult from illness, injury, or the presence of toxic substances. Mothers who have no prenatal care or who abuse alcohol or drugs increase the risk of cerebral palsy in their infants.

The incidence of cerebral palsy is generally estimated to be between 1 and 2 per 1,000 births. Approximately 7,000 to 9,000 children are born annually with some form of cerebral palsy. Another 1,500 preschool-age children acquire it, often as the result of head injury from abuse or accident. Incidence figures are sometimes difficult to ascertain, because many mild cases go undiagnosed or are unreported.

The range of disability for persons with cerebral palsy varies greatly and is dependent upon the extent of brain dysfunction. Persons may have mild, moderate, or severe degrees of involvement with all types of cerebral palsy. Early symptoms of cerebral palsy are variable. In milder cases, the condition may not be diagnosed until the child reaches school age. Generally, the more severe the condition, the earlier it can be detected.

Many different conditions fall within the broad terminology of "cerebral palsy," and there are considerable differences in descriptive terminology in the literature. The types of cerebral palsy can, however, be broadly divided into three major categories.

Spastic cerebral palsy results from dysfunction primarily in the motor area of the cerebral cortex, where voluntary motor activities originate. When this area is injured, or when it is improperly developed, it cannot regulate or coordinate neural stimulation to the muscles of the body. The result is hypertonia, or abnormally increased muscle tone in the affected muscles. Nerves in the motor areas of the cerebral cortex stimulate or inhibit contractions of muscles in specific areas of the body. The particular sites of brain damage and the extent of damage account for the differences seen in the parts of the body affected by spastic cerebral palsy. Increased spasticity can significantly reduce muscle efficiency and can make both simple and complex motor tasks difficult or impossible.

With mild to moderate spastic cerebral palsy, the person's gait is often awkward, and balance is impaired. Spasticity in the muscles of the legs and feet may lead to toe-walking or walking with the toes and knees turned inward. In severe cases, certain muscle groups may be entirely dysfunctional, and the person may not be able to stand or walk at all.

Both gross motor and fine motor activities can be affected. Gross motor activities, such as walking, sitting, standing, and simply maintaining head control, are impaired. A person with spastic cerebral palsy may also have considerable difficulty using her hands and fingers, may have difficulty in using her mouth and tongue to formulate speech, and may have vision problems due to weakness and/or lack of control of muscles of the eyes.

The presence of primitive reflexes, such as the ATNR (Asymmetric Tonic Neck Reflex) and other strong infantile reflexes, is common in cerebral palsy. The persistence of such reflexes over long periods of time may interfere with many normal activities and may produce scoliosis, a malformation of the spine.

Weakness of the diaphragm muscle makes the production of sounds difficult. An inability to force air out of the lungs can also lead to frequent respiratory infections. This is particularly problematic when food is inhaled while eating and cannot be coughed out. Impairment of the muscles used in chewing and swallowing also make eating or feeding difficult.

Tightness of the bowel may lead to chronic constipation, with a risk of bowel impaction.

Athetoid cerebral palsy is thought to be caused by damage to the basal ganglia, located toward the center of the brain, and related structures, causing involuntary muscle movements, varying degrees of muscle weakness, and hypotonia (lack of muscle tone). It is estimated that 20 to 40% of persons with cerebral palsy have the athetoid type.

Athetoid cerebral palsy is characterized by slow, writhing, involuntary, and uncontrolled muscle movements accompanied by muscle weakness. Movements are often irregular and unpredictable and include spasmodic contractions of individual muscles, such as jerks and twitches, or slow, smooth, writhing, and undulating movements. Persons with athetoid cerebral palsy often have severe difficulty with head control, and many cannot sit without being supported or propped.

In mild to moderate cases of athetoid cerebral palsy, the person may walk with a stumbling, lurching, uncoordinated gait. Pervasive muscle weakness may interfere with and, at times, totally prevent many motor activities. Persons with spastic and athetoid types of cerebral palsy together comprise between 75 to 80% of all cases. Many persons with cerebral palsy exhibit characteristics of both types.

Ataxic cerebral palsy may occur when there is damage to the cerebellum, the large area at the base of the brain that controls balance and coordination. Ataxic cerebral palsy is characterized by disturbances in balance and depth perception. People with ataxia may display varying degrees of imbalance and lack of coordination. They may stumble, fall, or walk into objects or furniture, and may have difficulty with eye coordination and depth perception. Their motor behaviors may be similar in appearance to symptoms of being intoxicated, and many persons with ataxic cerebral palsy are unfairly accused, and even at times arrested, for intoxication. In severe cases, people cannot maneuver their bodies through space and therefore, cannot walk. Approximately 10% of persons with cerebral palsy have the ataxic type.

While the term cerebral palsy broadly identifies a group of conditions, other medical terminology is often used to more specifically describe individual conditions. For example, the prefixes "hemi-," "di-," "para-," "bi-," and "quadra-" describe the involved portions of the body. The term "plegia," which translates as "paralysis," refers to the severe motor limitations of some persons with cerebral palsy. The term "paresis," which means weakness, is also used and refers to the characteristic muscle weakness found in most types of cerebral palsy. Abroms [1980b] defines some common diagnostic categories:

- *Spastic hemiplegia* refers to cerebral palsy of the spastic type affecting one side of the body only, with the arm generally more involved than the leg, and affecting the right side about twice as often as the left. "Hemi" literally means half.

- *Diplegia* refers to cerebral palsy in both legs, with little or no involvement of the arms or upper body. This may also be referred to as "paraplegia." (This is not the same as the paralysis in the lower half of the body that results from spinal cord injury.)

- *Spastic quadraplegia* refers to cerebral palsy of the spastic type, with all four limbs affected, but the legs generally more affected than the arms. Spastic quadraplegia is among the most commonly diagnosed types of cerebral palsy.

- *Dyskinesis* is a term that is often used synonymously with "athetoid" or "athetosis," as defined above.

Cerebral palsy is most often congenital, or present at birth. The specific cause cannot generally be determined. Many factors are thought to be common contributors to cerebral palsy, including prenatal infection such as rubella or cytomegalovirus (CMV), RH incompatibility, deprivation of oxygen, or head injury during birth. Cerebral palsy can also result from trauma during a long, difficult birth process, although it has also been suggested that difficulty in birthing may be a result of the cerebral palsy rather than the cause of it. Cerebral palsy may also be acquired by young children as a result of head injury from abuse or accident, from infections such as meningitis or encephalitis, or as a result of severe convulsions associated with high fever.

Children with cerebral palsy frequently have speech disorders due to poor control of the muscles involved in talking. Speech may be slurred, slowed, and difficult to understand. In the most severe cases, the child may be unable to speak. Alternative communication systems, such as signing, symbolic communications systems, or electronic speech devices, may provide a means of communication for the nonspeaking individual.

Associated Complications

Cerebral palsy is a disorder of motor functions. However, some persons with cerebral palsy have other disabilities as well, usually as a result of insult or damage to other areas of the brain. While the following conditions may be present in persons with cerebral palsy, they are not symptoms of cerebral palsy, but are indicators of a separate disabling condition.

- *Mental retardation.* It is estimated that from 35 to 50% of persons with cerebral palsy are also mentally retarded to some degree. However, it is incorrect to assume that someone with cerebral palsy is also retarded, even if they are severely affected with cerebral palsy. At least 50% of persons with cerebral palsy are within the normal and above average ranges of intelligence. Unfortunately, the sometimes unusual-looking behaviors and contorted speech patterns of persons with severe cerebral palsy have, in the past, led to their being misdiagnosed as mentally retarded, and subsequently institutionalized.

- *Epilepsy.* Studies have indicated that approximately 30% of persons with cerebral palsy also have some form of epilepsy. Persons with hemiplegia have been found to be the most vulnerable to seizure conditions.

- *Visual and hearing deficits.* Some individuals with cerebral palsy have hearing and visual disorders. Persons with cerebral palsy should be routinely screened for these problems. Strabismus, or crossed eyes caused by involvement of the muscles in the eyes, is fairly common in individuals with spastic cerebral palsy.

Early Identification

Cerebral palsy should be detected and diagnosed as early as possible to ensure optimum intervention. The early symptoms of cerebral palsy are variable. In milder cases, the effects are minimal, and the condition may not become apparent until the child is school age. Generally, the more severe the condition, the earlier it can be detected.

Child welfare workers must be skilled at recognizing the early indicators of cerebral palsy in populations of abused and neglected infants and children. This can ensure optimum early intervention. The following conditions might indicate cerebral palsy and would warrant a referral for assessment and diagnosis.

Abnormal Muscle Tone

Infants with cerebral palsy may exhibit either *hypotonia*, a significant lack of muscle tone characterized by loose, flaccid muscles and extremities, or *hypertonia,* an excessive degree of muscle tone characterized by tightness, stiffness, rigidity of limbs, and constricted movement.

Infants with cerebral palsy of both the spastic and athetoid types are typically hypotonic, lacking muscle tone, for the first few months of life. Spasticity will become evident around 4 to 5 months, or around 2 to 3 months in severe cases. Typical signs of hypertonia in infants related to spastic cerebral palsy might include the following:

- Keeping one or both hands tightly fisted or keeping the thumb clenched inside the closed fist, if the child is over 4 to 5 months old.

- Tightness of the hips, making it difficult to separate the infant's legs to change a diaper.

- Keeping the legs in a fully extended position, or crossing the legs or ankles; kicking both legs in unison by bringing both knees up to the chest together, rather than the more normal alternating-leg, bicycle-style kicking.

- Evidence of lack of vision, inability to focus, or to track moving objects in an infant over 2 months.

- Tongue thrust, moving the tongue in and out of the mouth, excessive drooling.

- After the age of 3, the child does not talk, or the child's speech is slurred and garbled and cannot be understood. The child appears to lack the physical ability to form and produce sounds.

- A persistent strabismus, or crossing of the eyes.

The most typical signs of hypotonia, or lack of muscle tone, are delayed motor development and a generalized "heaviness" or "floppiness" of the body. Signs of hypotonia include the following:

- Infant slumps, wobbles, lurches; cannot hold own body steadily in position, if over 4 months; appears to have no strength.

- Infant may not be able to suck or swallow; chokes on food or formula; may not have strong sucking reflex.

- Infant or young child's movements may be jerky and uncontrolled; child may reach for things and either under- or overshoot an object, or the arm will appear to "fly out of control" and knock over the object the child is reaching for.

Abnormal Patterns or Delayed Motor Development

Delayed motor development may exhibit itself in numerous ways:
- Inability of a newborn, placed face down, to lift and turn its head to the side to avoid suffocation; failure to achieve head control by 3 months; by 5 months, failure to lift head and chest from a prone position when the child is on his stomach; persistence of a head lag if the child is more than 5 months (when pulling the child by the arms from a position lying on his back, the head falls or "lags" back toward the floor, rather than being held in line with the rest of the body).

- Inability to bear weight on legs when held in a standing position, if older than 5 months.

- Failure to reach for objects, or to transfer objects from one hand to the other, if older than 7 months.

- Collapsing forward when placed in a sitting position, or a rounded back when seated, if older than 8 months.

- Inability to roll from back to front, if older than 6 months.

- Inability to stand holding on to objects or furniture, if older than 10 months.

Abnormal patterns of motor development can refer to developmental milestones that are only partially reached or to differences in the infant's skill in mastering motor tasks using various parts of the body. For example:
- Persistent use of only one hand when playing with a toy, including reaching across the body to retrieve an object, rather

than reaching with the arm that is on the same side of midline as the object. Infants typically use both hands equally for the first 15 to 18 months of life, and they rarely reach across the midline.

- Good use of hands and arms, but drags legs. While many infants go through a stage of crawling on their stomachs, failure to progress to the more advanced use of the legs might be indicative of cerebral palsy.

- Trembling or inaccurate aim when reaching for an object may indicate athetoid cerebral palsy.

- Child walks and runs at age-appropriate time but is always clumsy, has poor balance, falls all the time, runs into walls and door frames, or trips, after the child has been walking long enough that he should exhibit good balance and coordination; this may be symptomatic of ataxic cerebral palsy.

- Persistent walking on toes, with the heels not touching the ground, in a child over 2 years.

Persistent Reflexes

- Persistence of the Asymmetric Tonic Neck Reflex (ATNR), also known as the "fencing posture." This reflexive posture results in one arm bent at the elbow and raised to the level of the ear, with the head turned toward the opposite arm, which is stretched straight out from the shoulder, as if the infant were involved in a fencing match. This normal reflex in infants generally disappears within the first few months of life. The persistence of this reflex after a few months may indicate cerebral palsy. Many older children with cerebral palsy cannot turn their heads toward center-front without the reflex taking over and being repeated in the opposite direction. The presence of the reflex makes it impossible for these children to bring their hands together at the midline, to face directly forward, or to roll over back to front. This also clearly interferes with self-feeding and object manipulation.

- Persistence of a strong reflex to arch the head and upper torso may also suggest cerebral palsy. If an infant develops a bald spot on the back of his head from lying on his back, this may be indicative of a strong tendency to arch backward.

- Young infants typically stand on their tiptoes when held in an upright position in an adult's lap. By the time children learn to walk, they should be able to put their feet flat on the floor with the heels down. If toe-walking persists, the child may have an exaggerated toe-walking reflex, indicative of cerebral palsy. If this condition is not corrected, the muscles and tendons of the lower legs may permanently constrict and shorten, interfering with normal walking.

Treatment and Prognosis

Cerebral palsy is not a degenerative disorder—there is no progressive worsening of the brain damage. The symptoms and effects of the condition can, however, worsen if proper medical management is not provided. The degree to which cerebral palsy will disable an individual is related to the provision of prompt, effective, and lifelong intervention.

Physical therapy is essential to help the individual learn to compensate for and control primitive reflexes, to maintain muscle strength and flexibility, to develop coordination and control, and, ultimately, to permit optimal development in other developmental domains as well. When physical therapy is not provided, the tendency in spastic cerebral palsy is for the muscles to constrict, tendons and ligaments to shorten, and eventually for the joints to "freeze," seriously restricting the range of movement. With athetoid cerebral palsy, muscles that are not regularly exercised will further weaken and atrophy, reducing their efficiency even more.

For some individuals, drug therapy can help spastic muscles relax. Even though the spastic condition is caused by brain dysfunction, stress in the environment and a state of emotional tension in the individual can exacerbate the degree of spasticity in the muscles. Many persons with spastic cerebral palsy may be taught relaxation techniques to lessen muscle spasm related to environmental stress.

Vision and hearing should be routinely screened and monitored. Many persons with cerebral palsy need glasses to assure proper vision.

Speech therapy is an important intervention for persons whose ability to form speech is affected. Many people with cerebral palsy are fully capable of language, but because of poor muscle control of the mouth, lips, and tongue, and the inability to push air from the diaphragm through the larynx, speech is exceedingly difficult. For persons who are severely involved, alternate communication systems such as Bliss Boards (symbolic communication systems), signing, or computerized "voice boxes" can provide them a means of communicating with other people. The individual's ability to make his or her needs known and to communicate with other people is essential to healthy psychological and social development. The person with cerebral palsy should be provided with a means of communicating with others.

Daily care of persons with cerebral palsy requires specialized training and knowledge. Feeding may be difficult and time consuming. Persons with cerebral palsy may have extreme difficulty chewing and swallowing, and there is a danger of aspirating food during eating. Caregivers must be taught proper feeding procedures and must recognize symptoms of upper respiratory distress.

Many people with cerebral palsy want to feed themselves and need assistance or special equipment in order to manage utensils. Even with assistance, eating may take a long time. However, self-sufficiency should be encouraged to whatever degree possible.

Because of the difficulty in eating, many people with cerebral palsy may not get adequate nutrition and may be underweight for body size. Foods should be prepared with high nutritional value and should be easy to eat.

Caregivers should also be taught physical play activities that encourage the proper use of the child's muscles, which increase flexibility and strength and which maintain a wide range of motion. Specialized leisure time, play, and educational activities should be provided that are appropriate for each individual's physical ability and that take into consideration the level of cognitive ability, to assure sufficient cognitive stimulation.

Case Example

Maria was 4 months old. Her mother, Lydia Hernandez, had been referred to the child welfare agency several months before she delivered Maria because of questionable care of her 2-year-old daughter, Stella. With the worker's help, Lydia had improved her care of Stella, and managed reasonably well when the baby arrived.

Maria was a happy baby who seldom cried unless she was hungry or upset. Yet, she flopped around when anyone picked her up, and at 2 months, she couldn't hold her head up unassisted. When the worker saw the baby at 4 months, she was lying on her back on a blanket on the floor. Both legs were straight and rigid, and Maria's hands were tightly fisted, with the thumbs clenched inside. When excited, she flailed her tightly fisted hands on rigid arms in a jerky and exaggerated manner in front of her face. She kicked as if her legs were tied together at the knees and ankles, drawing both knees to her chest and then straightening the legs, digging her heels into the floor. Her smile was large and infectious, and she responded to interpersonal contact with expressive smiles and vigorous excited flailing of her arms and legs. She became excited whenever her mother appeared, or when people talked to her. Her mother said she had a good appetite, but feeding her was difficult; she had trouble sucking and her thrusting tongue often got in the way of the spoon.

The caseworker recognized Maria's symptoms as typical of cerebral palsy and referred her for diagnostic assessment. The attending physician confirmed spastic quadriplegia and referred Maria immediately for physical therapy and infant stimulation. The baby's responsiveness to other people, direct eye contact, and interactive nature suggested that, despite her considerable physical disability, she could potentially have normal intelligence, even though it was still too early to know. However, the caseworker's early recognition of Maria's condition assured that the baby would receive the necessary services to help her to develop to her potential.

EPILEPSY

Epilepsy, or more appropriately, "the epilepsies," refers to a group of disorders whose symptoms usually include seizures, which are symptoms of abnormal chemical/electrical phenomena in the brain [Abroms 1980a].

Before the role of the brain in seizure conditions was understood, it was thought that persons with epilepsy had been "seized" or possessed by the devil or other spirits; hence, the word "seizure" was used. Many people with seizure disorders were put to death or ostracized. It is now known that epilepsy can be hereditary or may be acquired through various insults or trauma to the brain. It is generally estimated that approximately 1 in 100 persons have some type of seizure disorder.

Many factors are known to contribute to acquired (nonhereditary) epilepsy. The most common are prenatal infections, alcohol or drug use during pregnancy, radiation during pregnancy, complications in labor and delivery with anoxia (deprivation of oxygen), direct head trauma, metabolic disorders, infections, diseases with high fever, and direct head injury from accidents or child abuse.

Generally, a seizure disorder results when some metabolic or structural abnormality temporarily or permanently changes the electrical stability of a group of neurons in the brain. The affected tissue is called the "focus." A seizure results when this area of instability spreads electrical stimulation inappropriately to other nearby neurons in the brain. The uncontrolled, abnormal firings of the neurons creates symptoms that are related to the particular area of the brain affected. Damage to different areas of the brain results in different patterns and types of seizures.

Epileptic seizures may be characterized by a broad range of symptoms, including alteration of consciousness, feelings, behavior, autonomic function (sweating, paleness, redness); somatic sensations (tingling hands); and motor activity. There are dozens of different types of seizure disorders. The most common are described below.

Generalized Tonic-Clonic Seizures

The generalized tonic-clonic seizure (previously known as grand mal) is also referred to as a major motor seizure. Tonic-clonic epilepsy may either be genetic or acquired. One type of tonic-clonic epilepsy is inherited as an autosomal dominant and is therefore present to some degree in nearly half of the members of an affected family. In a percentage of these persons, on an EEG (electroencephalogram) an abnormality will be present, but the patient will have no seizures.

A generalized tonic-clonic seizure normally occurs in two phases. During the tonic phase, the individual will suddenly lose consciousness, fall, or slump over. Air rushes from the lungs and he or she may scream or cry. The motor centers of the brain send a bombardment of electrical stimuli to the muscles of the body, which become rigid and stiff. Contraction of the muscles of the bowel and bladder may produce incontinence. The diaphragm muscles may also contract, and the individual may stop breathing, perhaps becoming cyanotic (blue from lack of oxygen).

During the second phase, called the clonic phase of the seizure, the muscles alternately contract and relax. This produces the jerking, sometimes violent thrashing that is often associated with tonic-clonic seizures. "Frothing" or excess salivating may occur as the individual begins to breathe again. A tonic-clonic seizure usually lasts from three to five minutes, and then the individual will regain consciousness. The aftereffects of a seizure may include headache, drowsiness, and a period of prolonged sleep.

Once a tonic-clonic seizure begins, it must run its course. The person should not be restrained, nor should anything be forced between the person' teeth. Well-meaning but untrained individuals can actually tear ligaments and break the bones of the person they are trying to help by trying to restrain them during a seizure. The person may inhale objects placed in the mouth, causing strangulation. Statistics show that the potential of harm far outweighs the efficacy of putting something between the person's teeth.

Appropriate interventions include loosening clothing and putting something soft under the person's head. Turning the person on his side or stomach will facilitate the flow of saliva from the mouth and will prevent blockage of the air passage by the relaxed tongue. Sharp objects and furniture should be removed from the area to prevent injury. Medical attention should generally be sought. If the seizure lasts more than a few minutes, or if one seizure is followed immediately by another, it should be considered a medical emergency. Unabated seizures of this type can lead to brain damage. Finally, having the person regain consciousness to a large group of staring spectators should always be avoided.

Most tonic-clonic epilepsy can be controlled by medication. Well-controlled childhood seizures may be outgrown by late adolescence, and the individual can maintain a seizure-free state without medication. In some cases, however, the biological changes during puberty may bring about a seizure condition for the first time in predisposed individuals.

Absence Seizures

There are several types of absence seizures with differing symptoms and prognoses. The most common was previously called petit mal. During this type of absence seizure, the individual has a momentary lapse of consciousness. He may blankly stare straight ahead and cease all movement and speech. There may be a rhythmical fluttering of eyelids and, at times, some finger or facial movements. If the individual is standing or sitting up, he will generally remain so and will not fall or slump over. At times, the person will just "stop what she's doing," with her body in position, until the seizure is over. One mother noted her daughter had a seizure while brushing her hair—she stopped, stared off into space with the brush in hand, high above her head, poised, and ready to use. She remained this way for several seconds, then resumed her brushing. The seizure generally lasts for 10 seconds or less; however, some persons with absence seizures may have between 50 and 200 seizures per day.

Absence seizures are often mistaken for daydreaming or inattentiveness. This type of epilepsy usually begins after age 3 and is most commonly seen in girls in the 5- to 9-year age range. Occasionally, seizures may begin during adolescence. In more than 70% of the cases, absence seizures cease by the time the child is 18 years old. If other types of seizures are present as well, it is less likely the absence seizures will be outgrown. Other types of absence seizures may be present in adults.

No intervention is possible during the seizure. However, if you are with a person for long periods of time, the frequency and duration of the absence seizures should be noted and reported. Often the physician or psychologist with case management responsibility will never witness a seizure and must rely on others for a description of the condition. This information, sometimes combined with abnormal EEG findings, will confirm the diagnosis of absence seizures. The most typical symptoms are repeated short "daydreaming" spells, a seeming inability to hear complete sentences or to follow directions, and repeated blank stares.

Some types of absence seizures can be well controlled by medication. However, if undiagnosed and untreated, the repeated lapses of consciousness may have significant effects. Untreated individuals may miss a significant amount of what goes on around them, and as a result, their ability to attend and learn may be negatively affected. In addition, emotional problems may result from a caregiver's anger at what appears to be an individual's inattentiveness, unresponsiveness, and apparent refusal to listen.

Psychomotor Seizures (Complex-Partial Seizures)

This type of seizure varies a great deal in appearance. It is often mistaken for emotional disturbance or other psychological disorders. While the symptoms of the seizure vary significantly from person to person, a single individual will display similar symptoms and behaviors during all seizures. These behaviors are often referred to as "stereotyped" behaviors.

There are both psychological and motor components related to this seizure condition. The seizure often begins with a sudden arrest of activity, with staring and a blank, dazed facial expression. The individual does not lose consciousness, but there is a "clouding of consciousness." The person seems "foggy" and does not appear to be clearly in touch with his environment.

Repetitive, automatic, and purposeless behaviors are frequent. These include inappropriate motor behaviors such as pacing, foot tapping, lip smacking, chewing movements, playing with nearby objects, and incoherent or irrelevant speech. Physical symptoms of stomach distress (including vomiting) and headache may at times accompany seizure.

The seizure may also be accompanied by strong emotional outbursts of anger or fear. The individual may swear, yell, physically strike out, and display an anger that does not seem to be appropriate for the situation. At other times the individual becomes fearful and anxious. It is for these reasons that psychomotor seizures are sometimes misdiagnosed as psychological or behavioral problems.

A psychomotor seizure may last anywhere from minutes to hours. When the seizure is over, the person generally remains lethargic and may sleep for a long period of time. The individual may have a partial, clouded memory of the seizure and of his behavior and generally will be confused. Youths with psychomotor seizures may have some awareness of their behavior and may apologize later, suggesting "I don't know why I do that."

Psychomotor seizures are less well controlled by medication than many other types of epilepsy. Individuals having the seizure should be monitored to ensure that they do not harm themselves or other people. It is most important that other people not respond to their angry outbursts with reciprocal anger; individuals with psychomotor seizures are not in control of their actions. Behavior outbursts must be viewed as a symptom of the seizure, and the individuals should be dealt with in a calm, reassuring, supportive fashion.

A substantial number of people with psychomotor epilepsy remain undiagnosed. They may develop secondary behavior problems resulting from the negative responses generated by other people in response to inappropriate behaviors displayed during seizures. They may be referred to as "crazy," "uncontrollable," or "dangerous"—labels that do not build positive self-esteem.

Case Example

Steve was 13 years old when the child welfare worker was assigned his case. Steve's family had received services from the agency when Steve and his younger sister, Mindy, were in preschool. At the time, the children were found to be neglected. Steve's mother had remarried shortly afterward, the care of the children had improved, and the case was closed. The current case opening was a referral from the juvenile court. Steve was reported to be "out of his parents' control," was truant from home and school, and had reported to court officials that his parents "beat the crap out of me." While there was no evidence of current or past bruises or scars, the court referred the case to the child welfare agency for assessment. Steve later admitted that his parents yelled a lot, but they had never beat him, and he must have been mad when he said it.

When the worker met with the family, they reported that at about age 9, Steve had developed "an attitude" that had gotten worse over time. The family asked whether Steve could be placed in a special school where he could be controlled and "taught some manners." The worker asked the family to describe Steve's behavior. They said he had "moods" and violent temper tantrums, often over nothing at all. When he was like that, there was no talking to him, and no settling him down. He would storm around the house, shout at them, scream at them, insult them, swear at the top of his lungs, kick things, and stomp his feet. They said he looked like he was possessed. At first, his family tried to talk to him and find out what was bothering him, but he wouldn't listen. They said he acted like he didn't even hear them. He said cruel things to them, and they were afraid he would hurt his younger sister. The worker asked if he ever had these moods anywhere else but home. The mother said he'd had several in school, enough to get him suspended several times. She also said that Steve was so angry at the school for punishing him that he now refused to go at all.

The worker asked about Steve's history. The family said that up until the age of 9, Steve had been a good child. The worker asked about his medical history, and the family couldn't remember his having any special problems. The worker asked whether there had been any stresses or problems in the family when Steve was 9. Again, they couldn't think of any.

The worker asked how long Steve's "moods" lasted. The mother said usually anywhere from an hour to half a day. She then said, "It just seems like he wears himself out. He winds down, and when it's over, he almost always goes to sleep for a good while." His mother then said, "Don't get me wrong; I think Steve's still a pretty good boy. When he's not in a mood, he's helpful and can be very pleasant. And I suppose he still has some of the morals we taught him, because he always acts real sorry later for cussing and acting up. But it must not stick, because it doesn't keep him from doing it the next time."

The worker recognized the pattern of Steve's behavior as possibly being psychomotor epilepsy. She asked the family if they could think of anything else Steve did during his moods, any repetitive motor behaviors with his feet, his hands, or his mouth. The family said he always stomped his feet. His mother also said that he drummed his fingers on the table top—enough that it almost drove her crazy.

The caseworker suggested to the family that a medical problem could be contributing to Steve's behavior and asked the family's permission to make a referral to a pediatric neurologist. Steve was diagnosed with psychomotor seizures. They were partially controlled with medication. Steve's parents and school personnel were counseled to deal with Steve's condition, and Steve was referred to a developmentally oriented youth group at the mental health center.

Other Seizure Conditions

In addition to these three major types of seizure conditions, two others should be mentioned because of their frequency in young children.

Infant myoclonic epilepsy is characterized by the sudden flexion of the infant's neck, trunk, and thighs with forward extension of the upper limbs. Myoclonic seizures look very much like the sudden full-body jerks that often occur just as we begin to drift off to sleep. The onset of infantile myoclonic seizures is usually between 6 to 12 months of age, but they may appear as early as 2 months. Myoclonic seizures may be frequent (several times a minute) and last for long periods of time (up to many weeks). These seizures in infants are usually a symptom of some neurological disease, and most infants exhibit subsequent symptoms of brain damage with mental retardation. Many affected infants have a shortened life span.

Finally, *febrile seizures* occur in conjunction with high fever in young children. This generalized seizure condition is usually limited to the duration of the fever, but may occasionally progress to other forms of epilepsy. It is important to refer a child who has had a febrile seizure to a physician for examination and possible treatment. The physician may prescribe anticonvulsant medication for a period of time to prevent additional seizures and to reduce the likelihood of having seizures later in life.

Treatment Interventions

Several drugs are used to control seizures. They include Dilantin, Tegretol, Depekane, Zarontin, Valium, phenobarbital, and others. Most anticonvulsant medications are central nervous system depressants and therefore may produce drowsiness, lethargy, and difficulties in concentration.

There are other more serious complications that are sometimes produced by anticonvulsant drugs, including digestive disorders, anemia, hyperactivity and irritability, skin eruptions, kidney and liver dysfunction, loss of motor coordination, double vision, slurred speech, sleep disturbances, and loss of appetite. The adjustment of drug levels in persons with epilepsy is an ongoing process, and the objective is to produce the greatest degree of seizure control with the fewest negative side effects. The efficacy of medications and their toxicity may also change over time. Drug intervention must be closely monitored by a physician.

Approximately 50% of persons with epilepsy can expect to be seizure free with proper medication. For another 30%, the frequency and/or duration of their seizures are significantly reduced. For approximately 20%, drug intervention does not significantly affect the duration or frequency of the seizures.

It has also been noted that learning disabilities are more common among children with epilepsy than in the general population. Special education interventions should be provided.

Despite the advances in medical knowledge, there remains a stigma about seizure conditions. Persons with epilepsy are sometimes discriminated against unnecessarily in job selection; a well-controlled seizure condition will usually not affect job performance or ability. However, some persons with seizure conditions cannot drive without posing a risk to themselves and others, and some occupations, such as construction on high-rise buildings or operation of certain machinery, can be dangerous for persons with epilepsy.

The stigma that often surrounds epilepsy may also contribute to psychological problems for persons with seizure disorders. Seizures may be frightening to the individual and are often frightening to people who witness them. With many seizures, a person may display erratic or embarrassing behaviors and a loss of control. Negative and inappropriate responses from people who witness a seizure can contribute to self-consciousness and lowered self-esteem. Caseworkers should be conscious of the sometimes frightening nature of seizures and of the social stigma and prejudice that often surround seizure conditions. They should be supportive and reassuring to the affected children and their families and should not overreact with inappropriate fear or anxiety.

The child welfare worker should recognize the following symptoms of epilepsy and should refer children suspected of having seizure conditions for medical evaluation:

- Children may have absence seizures if caregivers report that they often stare into space, don't hear half of what they are told, never listen, daydream continually, can't follow directions, seem to be in a fog or "spaced out," or stop what they are doing for several seconds in a "freeze frame," and then spontaneously resume where they left off.

- Children who are reported to have episodes of either emotional or behavioral outbursts accompanied by "strange" motor movements should be screened for psychomotor epilepsy. These seizures differ from other behavior or emotional problems in that there may not appear to be a logical precipitant for the emotional outburst, and the symptoms of the disturbance are stereotypic.

- If caregivers report that their infants' bodies "jerk" hard, the infants should be evaluated for evidence of myoclonic seizures.

MENTAL RETARDATION

The term "mental retardation" comes from the Latin word *retardare*, which means to be delayed or late. Mental retardation refers to the significant delays in cognitive, social, emotional, and physical development that are symptomatic of a wide variety of underlying conditions and syndromes.

Syndromes in which mental retardation is common include fragile-X syndrome, Down's syndrome (Trisomy 21) and many other genetic abnormalities, hydrocephalus, microcephaly, phenylketonuria (PKU), metabolic disorders, and others. Most often, however, a specific condition causing the mental retardation cannot be identified. Therefore, the term mental retardation is generally used as a broad diagnostic classification when significantly delayed development in all domains is the only symptom that can be clearly identified.

It is misleading to presume that persons who have mental retardation constitute a homogeneous group. There is wide variation in the degrees of developmental delay included under the broad classification of mental retardation. Mental retardation is generally subdivided into four categories to assist in classification: mild, moderate, severe, and profound. Each classification represents an increasing degree of delay in development and adaptive ability.

Hundreds of possible contributing factors have been associated with mental retardation. Some of these are more likely to result in severe or profound mental retardation: they include genetic factors, metabolic disorders, severe birth injury and trauma, severe prenatal infections, anoxia (lack of oxygen), head injury from an accident or abuse, and Rh incompatibility. However, only about 10% of persons with mental retardation fall into the severe and profound ranges.

In approximately 70% of cases, the cause of retardation cannot be determined. This is particularly true for persons with mild mental retardation. Environmental factors such as inadequate nutrition, lack of environmental stimulation, and prenatal exposure to drugs and alcohol are thought to be important contributing factors to mild mental retardation.

Approximately 3 in 100 individuals, or 3% of the total population, have some degree of mental retardation. Of these, approximately 90% fall into the mild range; 7% in the moderate range; and 3% in the severe and profound ranges.

Clinical Description

Mental retardation is defined by the American Association of Mental Retardation (AAMR) as follows:

> Mental retardation refers to substantial limitations in present functioning. It is characterized by significantly subaverage intellectual functioning, existing concurrently with related limitations in two or more of the following applicable adaptive skill areas: communication, self-care, home living, social skills, community use, self-direction, health and safety, functional academics, leisure and work. Mental retardation manifests before age 18 [American Association of Mental Retardation 1992].

"Substantial limitations" is further defined as scoring a minimum of two standard deviations below the mean on I.Q. tests and adaptive behavior assessments.

Intelligence

Intelligence is cognitive capacity. However, cognitive capacity is not a simple construct. Our cognitive capabilities are determined by the interaction of many different functions, including memory, analytic ability, perspective-taking ability, ability to synthesize information, symbolic reasoning, visual-spatial conceptualization, and others. Different strengths and weaknesses within the various cognitive functions are the basis for assessing cognitive capacity, or intelligence. Variability of individual strengths and weaknesses in different areas of cognition also gives us a rich diversity of cognitive styles. When a person has pervasive limitations in most of the cognitive functions, however, problems in adaptive behavior are more likely, including limited social judgment, difficulty adapting to changing circumstances, poor self-care and protection, deficits in practical reasoning, and limited vocational performance.

Clearly, it is difficult to measure something as complex and fluid as human intelligence. Yet, standardized intelligence tests are useful tools to measure cognitive capability, and they have proven to be highly correlated with a person's ability to learn and use new information, particularly in an educational or school setting. However, I.Q. tests by themselves cannot always supply enough reliable information about a person's capacity to function in day-to-day living. This additional information is essential for proper assessment, accurate diagnosis, and relevant case planning. Measures of adaptive behavior provide additional tools to assess a person's life skills.

Adaptive Behavior

The addition of adaptive behavior assessment in the diagnosis of mental retardation is relatively recent. Previously, mental retardation was diagnosed solely on the basis of performance on standardized intelligence tests, which do not assess a person's mastery of daily living. Such a measure is important, since mental retardation typically results in developmental deficits in many areas of functioning. Utilizing standardized measures of adaptive behavior decreases the likelihood of misdiagnosis. For example, many children with learning disabilities perform poorly on standardized intelligence tests, often because of reading or auditory processing problems. However, they are quite normal in most areas of functioning. In the past, such children were often misdiagnosed as mentally retarded based on their I.Q. test scores. With the addition of adaptive behavior inventories as a required part of the diagnosis for mental retardation, such misdiagnosis is less likely to occur.

Adaptive behavior is broadly defined as "the effectiveness or the degree with which the individual meets the standards of personal independence and social responsibility expected of his age and cultural group" [Thain et al. 1980]. Certain areas of functioning are commonly included in a definition of adaptive behavior:

- Skills for meeting basic physical needs. These include eating, dressing, toileting, and personal hygiene.

- Skills for daily living, which include cooking, cleaning, laundry, shopping, home maintenance, travel, the ability to use money, and the ability to care for personal belongings.

- Social skills, including interpersonal relationship skills, the ability to cooperate, language and communication skills, the ability to initiate and carry out purposeful activities, understanding social roles, the ability to work, behaving appropriately in social situations, and the ability to assume responsibility.

When mental retardation was diagnosed solely on the basis of measured I.Q., many persons were inappropriately labeled and received inappropriate treatment and educational programming. By including adaptive behavior measurements in the diagnosis of mental retardation, we help to ensure that only those persons whose functioning is significantly delayed in all areas are diagnosed as mentally retarded. A good adaptive behavior assessment also delineates problem areas and areas of greater skill, which improves our ability to provide the proper interventions.

Comparable deficits in both intelligence and adaptive behavior are necessary for a diagnosis of mental retardation.

Levels of Mental Retardation

The general characteristics of persons in each category of mental retardation and the expected developmental and functioning abilities for each category are outlined below.

Mild Mental Retardation

In childhood, mild mental retardation is generally not clearly diagnosed until a child is of school age. During infancy and the preschool years, mildly mentally retarded children may progress in their motor, social, and emotional development close to the "slower" end of normal, but there are typically no serious developmental delays.

In general, higher order cognitive skills are most affected in persons with mild mental retardation. This includes abstract or hypothetical reasoning ability, the ability to perceive and accurately interpret subtle interpersonal or environmental cues, the ability to weigh and consider information in making judgments or solving complex problems, and in understanding the perspectives of others.

A person with mild mental retardation is likely to have considerable problems mastering academic skills. Generally, a person with mild mental retardation may learn basic reading, writing, and math skills to about the fourth grade level. Mild mental retardation has been referred to as "educable mentally retarded," which implies a capacity to learn some basic academic skills.

If there are no accompanying physical or emotional disorders, persons with mild mental retardation are often able to function independently in the community, provided the environmental demands are not too complex. They can work and support themselves and can manage most daily activities, but may need direction and supervision from others during times of crisis or in matters that require more complex skills. They may also need help to avoid being exploited. Some persons with mild mental retardation can be adequate parents, if they are taught proper child care and parenting skills, and if they are given adequate support.

It must be remembered, however, that the mild range of mental retardation encompasses a continuum of 15 points in I.Q. and comparable adaptive behavior skills. Persons at the upper end of the range (I.Q. 70) will typically have more skills and potential for independent functioning than do persons who are closer to the lower end of the range (I.Q. 55). We must also remember that people with mild mental retardation are more like than unlike other people, and they are susceptible to all the emotional and psychological needs and problems we may see in persons falling into the "normal" or "above average" range of intelligence and adaptive behavior.

Moderate Mental Retardation

Moderate mental retardation can generally be diagnosed during infancy and early childhood. Sensorimotor development is often significantly delayed. Moderately retarded children, for example, may sit up at 12 months, walk at 2 years, be toilet trained at 4 years, and learn to talk at 6 years.

Persons with moderate mental retardation have sometimes been referred to as "trainable." The implication is that, while they do not possess academic potential, they are able to learn to perform many routine tasks. With appropriate training and supervision, persons with moderate retardation can learn to feed, toilet, bathe, and dress themselves; to assist in maintaining a living environment; and to perform functional work tasks, usually in a closely supervised or sheltered setting. Persons with moderate mental retardation can often live successfully in community-based group home settings, with proper help and supervision from family members and/or staff. Independent community living is generally not possible.

As with mild mental retardation, there are variations in the functioning of persons with moderate mental retardation, depending upon which end of the continuum they fall. Moderate mental retardation also spans a range of 15 points in I.Q., from 55 to 40. A person with an I.Q. of 55 and comparable adaptive behavior, will generally be more similar in functioning to a person at the lower end of the mildly retarded range than to someone at the lower end of the moderate range.

Severe and Profound Mental Retardation

Severe and profound mental retardation can generally be diagnosed early in infancy. The developmental delays are significant in all developmental domains. Severely and profoundly retarded persons typically require full-time supportive care. Persons with severe and profound mental retardation do not develop and use language for communication. Some persons in the severely retarded range may use some words or combinations of words to communicate, but they do not develop basic language skills.

A small percentage may be taught some basic self-help skills, such as self-feeding and toileting, but most individuals will need routine assistance in even basic self-help tasks. Many persons who are severely or profoundly retarded have physical disabilities as well. Because of the multiple physical factors that often accompany severe and profound mental retardation, including serious genetic abnormalities, many do not survive infancy or childhood.

Early Identification

The hallmark of mental retardation is delayed development that is comparable in all developmental domains—cognitive, physical, social, and emotional. If the child welfare worker knows the behaviors and abilities that represent the normal range for all developmental domains, recognizing delay is not difficult. The greater the discrepancy between development and chronological age, the more likely the child is mentally retarded. However, since many other factors can contribute to developmental delays, most psychologists do not diagnose children as mentally retarded until they are school age. Many children with early developmental delays have the capability to grow and develop, if given the proper intensive interventions. Therefore, any child with demonstrated delays in development should receive early intervention and developmental services, regardless of diagnosis.

Treatment and Intervention

Before any intervention program can be developed, a person with possible mental retardation should be thoroughly assessed and accurately diagnosed. This assessment should be performed by a competent psychologist who considers both I.Q. and adaptive behavior. Once an appropriate diagnosis has been made, an assessment of the person's skills and strengths, as well as service needs, should be completed. A comprehensive intervention program should then be provided to promote development, and improve adaptive behavior.

As is true with all developmental disabilities, the earlier the identification and intervention, the more we can maximize each person's functioning. Any intervention program should plan for developmental activities in all four developmental domains and should include the following components.

Education and/or Training

By definition, persons who are mentally retarded are slower in their development and in their rate of learning—but they do learn. The degree to which they will progress in any area will be limited by the degree of retardation; however, the way learning experiences are structured and presented can significantly influence how far, and how quickly, they can progress.

Research has consistently demonstrated that early, intense educational intervention, including infant stimulation, structured preschool experiences, and specialized school programming, can significantly promote and improve a child's cognitive and adaptive development. Activities in the home which provide structured and consistent stimulation are also helpful.

There are many technologies that have been developed to help children and adults with mental retardation acquire, generalize, and maintain skills in a wide variety of areas. Learning activities should be well planned and formalized using an Individual Education Plan (IEP) or Individual Habilitation Plan (IHP). Staff should be trained in specialized methods of teaching or training persons with mental retardation.

Physical and Health Care

Many syndromes include both mental retardation and physical disabilities that can restrict a person's mobility, ability to manipulate objects, self-help activities, and the capacity to interact with others. These physical conditions must be treated and managed. Physical therapy, medical care, and the use of prosthetic devices can minimize the effects of many physical disabilities and can enhance the individual's development of adaptive skills.

Each child with mental retardation should be routinely examined by a physician. Caregivers should know and recognize signs and symptoms of physical illness, since persons who lack verbal communication skills may have difficulty communicating illness or pain. Children with conditions that require medication and medical management should be treated by physicians who specialize in providing services to persons with developmental disabilities.

Social and Recreational Opportunities

It is often wrongly assumed that people with mental retardation don't have the same social and affiliative needs as other people, and they are often excluded and isolated from typical social and interpersonal experiences. Because their verbal communication skills may be limited, it is not unusual for other people to discount or ignore them. Isolation and exclusion have contributed to emotional problems, including depression, low self-esteem, and boredom in many people with mental retardation, particularly in the mild and high moderate ranges.

Structured recreational experiences, including games, activities, and outings into the community should be routinely provided. These opportunities can promote the development of relationships and the learning of useful social skills, as well as create a pleasant, nurturing environment.

Persons of all ages with mental retardation have the same basic needs for nurturing, stability, affection, intimacy, and affiliation as do all people. Family members and caregivers should assure that these social needs are recognized and addressed.

Normalization and Inclusion

An important concept in serving persons with mental retardation is normalization, which refers to providing a pattern of life that is as similar as possible to the normal, or typical, life of the rest of the population. Inclusion refers to routinely involving persons with mental retardation in typical life events and social experiences.

In the recent past, persons with mental retardation were segregated into very atypical living and social environments in institutions and in segregated schools. This was often justified as being in the best interests of the person with retardation. We now know that a lifetime of segregation often promotes further developmental retardation and makes integration into society impossible. Children with retardation who are raised in their own homes and communities not only progress further in all areas of development than children raised in institutional settings, but their adaptive behavior skills are better suited to functioning within the community environment. This is true for adults with mental retardation as well. In general, adults who are provided with a community-based living arrangement with proper services have a greater opportunity to develop appropriate skills and to function within the community.

Any intervention program for a person with mental retardation should include as many activities as possible in normal social, recreational, educational, and vocational environments. Unnecessary isolation and segregation should be avoided.

Case Example

Gregory, age 3 1/2, was referred to the child welfare agency by his Head Start teacher, who thought he was being neglected by his mother. Gregory was the youngest of five children cared for by a single mother. The Head Start teacher liked Gregory's mother, but thought her to be limited in her abilities.

Gregory had started coming to Head Start about three months earlier. He had been enrolled by a welfare department caseworker who was helping Gregory's mother explore job opportunities as part of her financial assistance grant.

The Head Start teacher reported that Gregory came to school hungry and dirty, and his clothes were not appropriate for the weather. He was not toilet trained, and he was often urine soaked, since his mother had him in training pants. The teacher also believed he was quite delayed in his development.

The caseworker met with the Head Start teacher in the classroom. Together they observed Gregory and did a gross developmental screening. Gregory's gait looked like that of a child who had just learned to walk. He stumbled often and appeared to lack balance and coordination. He didn't seem to know what to do with the play equipment in the room, and he did not know how to climb. He generally used a full-hand palmar grasp, and only occasionally did he show good finger-thumb opposition. He tried to feed himself finger foods, but he would not hold a fork or spoon. He held a bottle but would not drink from a cup. He chose simple toys, such as colored beads, and he amused himself by placing them into a bucket and dumping them. He often wandered around the room picking up objects and dropping them. He did not play with other children. He knew several simple words, but he did not speak phrases or sentences. He was responsive to the Head Start teacher; he was affectionate and liked to be cuddled.

The worker and teacher together decided, giving him the benefit of the doubt, that Gregory's development was generally more typical of a 1- to 2-year-old than a 3 1/2-year-old. The caseworker made a referral to a psychologist who specialized in working with children with delays. The developmental assessment confirmed that Gregory was, on average, functioning between 12 and 18 months of age. The psychologist suggested that, while Gregory was too young to make a final diagnosis, this represented a potentially moderate level of mental retardation and that specialized services were essential immediately. Gregory was transferred to the intensive early intervention preschool associated with the county Mental Retardation and Developmental Disabilities program.

Gregory's mother was also assessed and was determined to be functioning between low-normal and high-level mild mental retardation. She was linked with the proper services to provide her with in-home instruction on child care and the essentials of home management. A volunteer was assigned to help her twice weekly. Her other children were also assessed and found to be functioning at the low-normal/mildly retarded level of intelligence. The volunteer assisted Gregory's mother to improve her care of all her children.

The worker followed Gregory's development for six months. The Early Intervention Preschool indicated that he was progressing, albeit slowly, and that the mother was actively involved with the program. The volunteer was still involved and was committed to helping the family. Both the children and their mother referred to the volunteer as "Grandma." The preschool believed Gregory would always need some level of special education, and they assumed responsibility for his ongoing educational and developmental planning. The child welfare caseworker closed the case, since there was no further evidence of neglect, and the children were being monitored by other community professionals.

Fragile-X Syndrome

Fragile-X syndrome is the most common known inherited cause of mental retardation. It is a sex-linked disorder with an estimated incidence of 1 in 1,000 males. Females display the syndrome less frequently. Fragile-X syndrome was first identified in 1943 by Martin and Bell, who published a family pedigree that described a sex-linked form of mental retardation. The chromosome defect was first located and described in 1969, but the specific gene responsible for the syndrome was not identified until 1991.

Genetic transmission in fragile-X syndrome is similar to other X-linked chromosomal disorders, such as hemophilia and certain types of muscular dystrophy. All humans have 23 pairs of chromosomes. One of these pairs determines gender. Normal males have an XY chromosome pair, and normal females have an XX pair. In fragile-X syndrome, an X chromosome is malformed. Males who inherit this defective X chromosome always exhibit the syndrome. The syndrome is less frequently expressed in females, because they have a second X chromosome in the gender-determined pair, which is usually normal and appears to block or mediate expression of many of the symptoms. These women are called "carriers," since while they, themselves, exhibit no symptoms, the abnormal chromosome can be transmitted to their children.

The primary symptom of fragile-X syndrome is mental retardation. Most males with fragile-X syndrome exhibit moderate to severe mental retardation. Most females with fragile-X syndrome have normal I.Q.s, but they often have learning disabilities. However, 30% function in the borderline to mildly retarded range.

Autistic traits are also common in males with fragile-X. Common behaviors include avoidance of eye contact, hand flapping, self-injurious behavior such as hand biting, tactile defensiveness, unusual sensitivity to stimuli, and perseveration in speech and behavior. Hyperactivity, attention deficits, language delays with echolalic speech (repeating the speech of others), aggressive outbursts, and a pervasive lack of interpersonal responsiveness are also noted. Males with fragile-X also are more shy, socially withdrawn, emotional, and less energetic than males with mental retardation with other etiologies. Adaptive behavior appears to be similar to that of other persons with comparable mental retardation.

Physical features associated with fragile-X include a long, thin face with large, prominent ears, joint laxity, flat feet, cardiac abnormalities such as mitral valve prolapse, esophageal reflux, hypotonia (lack of muscle tone) and hyperextensibility of the joints, all suggesting an underlying connective tissue disorder. Infants with fragile-X have often been noted to have difficulty feeding, often resulting in failure to thrive.

Some children with fragile-X syndrome are misdiagnosed as autistic because of their autistic-like symptoms. However, most persons with autism do not have a fragile-X chromosome. Autism and fragile-X appear to remain distinct disorders, even though some of their symptoms are similar.

Children diagnosed with fragile-X should receive intensive early intervention to promote maximum development of both intelligence and adaptive behavior, although the prognosis for most is limited. Women can now receive genetic screening to determine whether they are carriers of the fragile-X chromosome. Genetic screening and counseling are recommended if a familial history of sex-linked mental retardation is noted.

Down's Syndrome (Trisomy 21)

The first clinical description of Down's syndrome was published in 1866 by a British physician named John Langdon Down. Down had observed that several of his patients who were mentally retarded all had fairly similar physical features, including facial features he thought resembled those of Mongolian or Oriental peoples. At the time, the term "idiot" (from the Greek *idios*, meaning peculiar or unique) was a common diagnostic category of mental retardation. Down named his syndrome "Mongolism" and referred to persons with the syndrome as "Mongoloid Idiots." As the English social structure of the time was strongly prejudiced against Oriental peoples, the term "Mongolism" quickly became derogatory. The syndrome is now widely referred to as Down's syndrome, or Trisomy 21, which more accurately reflects the nature of the disorder.

Down's syndrome results from an abnormality in chromosome formation. The normal human chromosome configuration is 46 chromosomes organized into 23 pairs. A trisomy is an abnormal grouping of three chromosomes instead of a normal pair. Most people with Down's syndrome have a trisomy of the 21st chromosome pair, and a total of 47 chromosomes. This trisomy most often occurs through an error in cell division during the development of reproductive cells. The result is the development of a sperm or egg cell that carries an extra chromosome. If this reproductive cell is fertilized during conception, the resulting embryo carries the extra 21st chromosome in all its cells, producing the syndrome. Hence, the formal name for the syndrome is Trisomy 21.

Approximately 3 to 5% of Down's syndrome cases result from a chromosome translocation. In a translocation, a broken-off portion of another chromosome attaches to the 21st chromosome, thereby changing its structure and its function. It is important to identify this group of individuals, since the translocated chromosome may have been transmitted by a parent who carries the chromosome abnormality, but who is developmentally normal. In such families the risk of recurrence of Down's syndrome in subsequent pregnancies is considerably higher (10 to 15%) than for the more typical trisomy (1%) [Bartoshesky 1980].

The incidence rate for Down's syndrome is approximately 1 per 700. Research shows that the risk of bearing children with Down's syndrome increases with maternal age. Estimates are approximately 1 in 1,500 for mothers age 25; 1 in 1,000 for mothers age 30; 1 in 350 for mothers age 35; and 1 in 50 for mothers age 40 and over. The risk is also higher for young teenage mothers. Down's syndrome appears to occur equally in male and female children and within all racial and ethnic groups.

Clinical Description

Children with Down's syndrome are most often identified at birth because of characteristic facial and physical features. However, positive identification of Down's syndrome should never be made without a chromosome analysis (karyotype) that confirms the presence of the chromosomal abnormality. In the past, some people who had similar facial features to persons with Down's syndrome were improperly diagnosed and placed in institutions, even though they were later determined to be of normal intelligence and ability.

Down's syndrome may be detected in the fetus through amniocentesis, wherein a sample of the amniotic fluid is extracted, and an assessment is made of individual cells to determine their chromosome configuration. This may be performed at the beginning of the second trimester of pregnancy. The most common clinical features of Down's syndrome are as follows:

- *Short stature.* Almost all persons with Down's syndrome are shorter than average and reach full height at about age 15. Typical height is around 5 feet.

- *Flat facial profile and flat nasal bridge.* Approximately 90% have flat faces and a flat, almost absent nasal bridge.

- *Hypotonia and hyperextensibility of joints.* Evident in approximately 80% of people with Down's syndrome. Hypotonia, or lack of muscle tone, is noted at birth and tends to improve as the child develops. Hypotonia and joint hyperextensibility tend to contribute to delayed motor development.

- *Slanted eyes with inner canthal folds (epicanthal folds).* These are present in approximately 80% of people with Down's syndrome.

- *Short neck with excess skin on back of neck.* The head seems to sit close to the shoulders, which often appear rounded.

- *Microcephaly.* The head is often smaller than normal and is typically flattened at the back.

- *Enlarged tongue and malformed, improperly placed teeth.* The malformations of the mouth and an enlarged tongue often result in protrusion of the tongue from the mouth.

- *Low-set and malformed ears.* The ears may be strangely shaped and are low on the sides of the head.

- *Transverse palmar crease.* Often referred to as a "simian crease." The "life lines" in the upper portion of the palm form a single linear crease across the palm.

- *Congenital heart disease and malformations.* Present in 40 to 60% of persons with Down's syndrome. Before the availability of open heart surgery, this constituted a major cause of death for infants with Down's syndrome. Corrective surgery has improved the prognosis for these children considerably.

- *Digestive malformations.* Persons with Down's syndrome may have problems with the stomach, esophagus, and digestive tract due to malformations in these organs.

- *High susceptibility to leukemia.* The incidence of leukemia in persons with Down's syndrome is estimated to be approximately 20 times greater than in the normal population.

- *Hearing deficits.* Hearing loss in some children with Down's syndrome contributes to delayed speech and language acquisition. Children should be screened to assure their hearing is not impaired.

- *Spinal cord malformation.* About 10% of individuals with Down's syndrome have a malformation of the cervical vertebrae called Atlantoaxial Dislocation. Without early identification and corrective surgery, strenuous physical activity can lead to cervical and central nervous system damage. All persons with Down's syndrome should be screened by x-ray for this condition.

- *Adolescent/sexual development.* Females with Down's syndrome may menstruate, and some have been known to bear children. Males are generally infertile and have low serum testosterone levels. Adolescent sexual development is typically incomplete.

- *Cognitive development.* Almost all persons with Down's syndrome are mentally retarded. The degree of retardation varies, ranging from mild to severe. The average level of cognitive development is in the moderately mentally retarded range. A few individuals with Down's syndrome have been identified within the low-normal range of intelligence.

- *Social development.* Many persons with Down's syndrome attain social and interpersonal skills that are more highly developed than would be expected for their general degree of mental retardation.

Prognosis and Treatment

At least 20% of infants with Down's syndrome are stillborn. While in the past, many children with Down's syndrome did not survive early childhood, advances in medical treatment and management of the associated physical conditions have reduced the rate of infant deaths.

The developmental level of persons with Down's syndrome is affected by many congenital and environmental factors. Individual assessment of each person with Down's syndrome is essential to determine areas of strength and service need. Many persons with Down's syndrome are relatively competent socially, despite intellectual deficits, and they are able to function reasonably well in a family or group home setting. Because most persons with Down's syndrome are not seriously physically disabled, many have been able to learn vocational tasks and can work in supervised or sheltered workshop settings. Most persons with Down's syndrome learn to talk and use language to communicate with others.

Studies have consistently demonstrated that children with Down's syndrome who are raised at home in nurturing and stimulating environments typically outperform children raised in institutional settings in their cognitive, adaptive, and social functioning. Early intervention, including infant stimulation and preschool programs, also contribute positively to the child's development. This is of particular importance for child welfare professionals who may have responsibility for permanency planning for these children. For children who cannot be maintained in their own home, adoption is the most appropriate placement.

The physical development of children with Down's syndrome is generally delayed. Speech and language acquisition are also delayed and may be related to hearing deficits. Some persons with Down's syndrome also display behavior disorders, including hyperactivity, autism, and other affective disorders. These disorders should be considered additional disabling conditions, not typical symptoms of Down's syndrome.

Life expectancy is reduced for persons with Down's syndrome. They also tend to show physical signs of aging earlier. Decreases in infant deaths are lengthening the statistical life expectancy. Still, the life expectancy is about 50 years.

Services

Children with Down's syndrome in the child welfare system will likely need the full range of developmental and supportive services. Young children should be cared for in family settings with supportive educational, recreational, and respite services. This will generally require linking the family to dependable community resources and supports. Children in need of permanent placement should be adopted. Community-based settings that combine supervised group home living with vocational training are appropriate for older youth with Down's syndrome. Placement into nursing care or other institutional settings should be avoided, unless the individual is severely or profoundly retarded, and requires constant care.

SPINA BIFIDA

S pina bifida is a congenital deformity of the spinal column. The defect occurs within the first six weeks of fetal development, when the cells that form the brain and central nervous system are in their early stages of development.

In spina bifida, the central nervous system cells forming the neural tube fail to fuse and close, usually at the lower end of the spine. The bony arches of the spinal column subsequently fail to develop properly, and they may also remain open. Portions of the central nervous system, including the spinal nerve cord fibers, the meninges (membranes that cover the nerves in the central nervous system), and parts of the autonomic nervous system, do not develop properly because of the defect. These neurological structures may also protrude through the open spinal column and be exposed in the midline region of the lower back. In myelomeningocele, which is the most serious of several types of spina bifida, neural transmission through the spinal cord may be interrupted and impaired.

There are many factors that can lead to spina bifida. The highest incidence occurs in England, Ireland, and Wales, and in persons with this ancestry. Spina bifida is rare among people of African or Asian ancestry. The wide variation in incidence rates among different races would suggest some genetic etiological factors. Genetic factors are thought to sensitize the developing embryo to the effects of some environmental influence during the first month of intrauterine life, creating a complex interaction of genetic factors and an environmental "trigger." Incidence rates are between 2 and 5 per 1,000 births. It is more common in girls than in boys.

While spina bifida cannot be prevented, it can be detected prenatally through amniocentesis. Substances that are not normally in the amniotic fluid may leak from the open spine. The presence of these substances in the amniotic fluid sample generally indicates a cystic defect. Spina bifida may also be detected by an ultrasound examination.

There are three main types of spina bifida: spina bifida occulta, meningocele, and myelomeningocele. Of these, usually only the myelomeningocele poses severe developmental problems for the child. However, as the first two types are also referred to as spina bifida, they should be mentioned.

Spina Bifida Occulta

The neurological deformity is limited to a small, bony defect in the vertebrae of the spinal column and can only be seen on x-ray examination. Most patients have no symptoms. There may be a dimple, a discoloration of the skin, or a growth of hair over the malformed vertebrae. Some persons may have mild motor weakness, or disorders of sphincter control, but these may not develop until later in life. Some studies suggest that as many as 25% of people have this benign form of spina bifida.

Meningocele

The bony defect in a meningocele is confined to a few vertebrae and is usually located in the sacral or lumbar (lower) regions of the spine. The defect, called a cyst or cele, consists of a sac of the meninges (the membranes covering the nerves in the spinal cord), which protrudes through the opening in the bony vertebra. This sac fills with cerebrospinal fluid. It is often covered by more or less intact skin, and the spinal cord and nerves are usually not involved. There is seldom weakness in the legs, lack of sphincter control, or any other neurological dysfunction. Surgical correction is necessary immediately after birth to prevent rupture of the sac and subsequent infection. The prognosis is good with surgical correction.

A secondary problem for persons with meningocele is hydrocephalus, which occurs in approximately 9% of affected persons. This is also surgically correctable, with a good prognosis.

Myelomeningocele

Myelomeningocele is the most severe form of the three types of spina bifida. It occurs four to five times more frequently than the simple meningocele. The defect consists of a wide opening in the spinal column, covering several vertebrae, usually in the lumbar or sacral region. A grapefruit-sized sac protrudes through the opening in the spine. The sac, formed by the meninges, contains spinal cord nerves and cerebrospinal fluid. The misplacement of spinal cord nerves typically impairs neural transmission and may affect many motor, sensory, and autonomic functions.

The degree of disability resulting from the myelomeningocele depends upon several factors, including the location of the malformation and the extent of involvement of neural tissues. While generally located in the lower areas of the spine, the defect may occasionally occur in the mid-back (thoracic), or even the neck (cervical) areas. The higher on the spine the defect occurs, the more likely there will be widespread and serious neurological dysfunction. The degree of disability from myelomeningocele may range from mild to severe, but a high percentage of people born with this type of spina bifida are seriously physically disabled.

Interruption of neurological transmission between the brain and the lower portions of the body may lead to paralysis, motor weakness, loss of motor control, impaired sensory functions, and autonomic nerve dysfunction in areas of the body that are typically innervated by nerves in the spinal cord below the level of the myelomeningocele.

Orthopedic problems such as hip dysplasia, "rocker-bottom" feet, and other deformities are caused by inconsistent innervation and stimulation to opposing muscle groups. This leads to unbalanced muscle tone and abnormal muscle tension on opposing muscles, creating disproportionate muscle development, and also bone and joint malformations. Some individuals are able to stand and walk with braces; others must use wheelchairs for mobility.

Persons with myelomeningocele often have difficulty controlling the bladder, which may lead to constant urinary dripping and failure of the bladder to empty completely. Retention of urine in the bladder for an extended period of time often leads to repeated urinary tract and bladder infections. When not treated, these may result in damage to the urinary tract or the kidneys. Historically, one of the largest causes of mortality for persons with spina bifida was kidney damage from untreated urinary infections. Poor innervation of the anal sphincter muscle and the bowel can lead to incontinence or to the retention of fecal matter in the lower bowel.

Hydrocephalus is an abnormal accumulation of cerebrospinal fluid in the cavities inside and around the brain. Hydrocephalus occurs in approximately 65% of persons with myelomeningocele. It results from malformations in portions of the spinal cord that occur in the head and neck area. Hydrocephalus may develop prenatally or immediately after birth. If it is untreated, it typically leads to brain damage and mental retardation. This is a serious problem, because prenatal hydrocephalus is difficult to treat. The infant with myelomeningocele may be born with serious brain damage due to prenatal hydrocephalus.

Some fetuses with myelomeningocele spontaneously abort prior to reaching full term. Difficult labor and delivery is common for children with myelomeningocele for several reasons. The child's head may be enlarged because of prenatal hydrocephalus. The child's lower limbs may be paralyzed and inappropriately positioned, and the birth position is often breech. The spinal deformity is susceptible to birth injury, including injury to the nerves in the spinal cord. The open myelomeningocele is susceptible to infection, including spinal meningitis. This can lead to additional central nervous system damage or death. Most children with myelomeningocele are in poor condition at birth and are more likely to be delivered with forceps, which can add risk to the child during the delivery. If it is known that the infant has myelomeningocele, a cesarean delivery may be used.

A percentage of children have pervasive neurological damage by the time they are born. Some do not survive. However, because of the wide variability of presentation of this condition, there are also many children born with normal cognitive abilities and manageable physical impairments, who can lead very normal lives, if they receive proper medical management.

Treatment and Management

Treatment for an infant with myelomeningocele begins immediately after birth. Medical intervention may be complex because of the multiplicity of problems that may be present, but prompt medical attention decreases the probability of infection or subsequent injury.

Surgery is often performed immediately to repair the defect and cover the open spine to prevent infection or additional injury. Surgical insertion of a shunt may also be necessary to treat hydrocephalus and prevent subsequent brain damage. A shunt is a tube that is inserted into the head cavity and extends through the neck into the chest cavity. Excess cerebrospinal fluid drains through this tube and is absorbed and disposed of by the normal body processes. These shunts must be evaluated periodically by physicians to assure that they do not become blocked, causing subsequent accumulation of spinal fluid and neurological problems.

Orthopedic deformities may be surgically corrected to minimize their negative effects. Prosthetic devices such as wheelchairs, braces, and other orthopedic aids can increase mobility. Ongoing medical attention must be provided, particularly in growing children, to manage orthopedic problems and promote development.

Individuals must be checked often for the presence of urinary infection. In the past, surgery was often performed to detach the urethra and attach it to an opening in the abdomen to permit continuous drainage. This procedure, called urinary tract diversion, requires major surgery and creates another medical condition that requires ongoing attention. More recently, the use of a nonsurgical procedure called intermittent catheterization has been adopted by many physicians for patients with myelomeningocele. A sterile catheter is used by the caregiver, or by the patient, to drain the bladder several times a day. This is currently the treatment of choice, as it is considerably easier than surgery, and it is more similar to normal bladder functioning.

An associated problem, however, is urinary tract infection that may result from unsterile catheters. The urinary infection may be quite advanced by the time it is diagnosed, since the person with myelomeningocele often lacks sensation in the lower body and cannot feel and report urinary pain typical of bladder infections. Regular urinary screening for infection, and antibiotic therapy when needed, can eliminate this problem.

Mental retardation in persons with myelomeningocele is generally the result of hydrocephalus or central nervous system infection. If these underlying conditions are controlled or prevented, the degree of mental retardation is not progressive. However, children who have had any degree of hydrocephalus must be fully evaluated to ensure that early developmental and educational planning include consideration of any special needs.

Persons with myelomeningocele who are also mentally retarded will have more difficulty being self-sufficient, particularly if mental retardation is severe. The effects of mental retardation in persons with myelomeningocele are the same as with other persons who have comparable degrees of intelligence and adaptive functioning. However, the need to manage the multiple physical conditions associated with the myelomeningocele may complicate the caregiving process.

AUTISM AND OTHER PERVASIVE DEVELOPMENTAL DISORDERS

Pervasive developmental disorders include a group of conditions characterized by severe and pervasive impairment in several areas of development and adaptive behavior, primarily reciprocal social interaction and verbal and nonverbal communication, or when stereotyped behavior, interests, and activities are present. These disorders are usually evident in the first few months to years of life. These disorders include autistic disorder, Rett's syndrome, childhood disintegrative disorder, Asperger's syndrome, and pervasive developmental disorder not otherwise specified (PDD) [American Psychiatric Association 1994]. Primary differentiating features are the age of onset of the symptoms and the typical developmental course.

Autism

Of all of the developmental disabilities, autistic disorder, often called autism, is one of the most difficult to understand and to diagnose. The symptoms of the condition may be quite variable, and a clear cause has not been determined.

Many behaviors displayed by persons with autism are also common in other conditions, such as mental retardation, schizophrenia, fragile-X syndrome, other pervasive developmental disorders, and deafness-blindness. As a result, arriving at a diagnosis of autism is often difficult, and misdiagnosis is common. The common use of the description "autistic-like" for some conditions further illustrates the high degree of uncertainty in determining who should be diagnosed with autism.

Autism was first identified and described by Leo Kanner in 1943, and he continued to study and publish about the disorder for many years

[Kanner 1973]. While a physician at Johns Hopkins University, Kanner recognized that a group of children who had been diagnosed "retarded," or "psychotic," had consistent and similar behavior patterns. These included indifference to other people, abnormal speech patterns or absence of speech, and a peculiar and stereotypic preoccupation with objects. It was these children's emotional remoteness and social withdrawal that prompted Kanner to name the syndrome "Early Infantile Autism," from the Greek word *auto*, which means "self." Kanner hypothesized that autistic children were unable to form the normal emotional bonds with other people and that the problem was probably present at birth.

Kanner also identified certain characteristics in the parents of children with autism, which he initially felt contributed to the onset of the disorder. He observed that many parents of autistic children appeared to be reserved and aloof and lacked warmth in their relationships. He described these parents as "cold, humorless perfectionists of above-average intelligence, detached." Many of the parents were committed and successful professionals.

While Kanner speculated about the relationship between these parental characteristics and the presence of autistic symptoms, he did not suggest that parental behavior alone caused autism in children. Kanner felt there were many factors to be considered as possible causes of autism. However, for many years following Kanner's initial publication, the preferred treatment for autism was family psychotherapy. This approach to treatment implied that the parents' own lack of emotional contact with their children contributed to the children's disabilities. As a result, parents of children with autism were often made to feel that they were responsible for their children's condition.

In retrospect, while Kanner's identification of autism as a distinct syndrome was diagnostically astute, his initial sample of children and their families was quite small, and his judgment regarding the role of parents in causing the disorder was premature. More extensive studies have illustrated that most parents of children with autism do not fit Kanner's early stereotype. Additionally, it is believed that the aloof behaviors seen in parents of these children may be related to the child's inability to interact emotionally with and rejection of the parent. Therefore, the conflicted and distant parent-child relationships are likely a result of the child's condition, rather than a cause of it.

Etiology and Incidence

Incidence figures for autism are difficult to obtain, because there is still little clinical reliability in diagnosis. Most researchers estimate the incidence of autism to be between 5 and 15 children per 10,000 births.

There appear to be no family, racial, or ethnic factors correlated with autism. Some research indicates that autism is four to five times more prevalent in boys than it is in girls, but girls with autism are more likely to be mentally retarded. There is some support for a genetic origin for the syndrome, and neurologic involvement is likely. Some youth with autism develop seizures, particularly during adolescence, and EEG abnormalities are common, even in the absence of seizures. However, a precise etiology for autism has not been determined.

Clinical Description

Autism is believed to be present at birth. There is typically no period of unequivocal normal development. However, some children's development may appear relatively normal for a year or two; the symptoms may not be obvious, or they may be so mild as to be overlooked or denied by parents. Some parents note that their infants were "strange" or "different," but they cannot always specify why.

Some infants with autism may cry less often, may appear content to be left alone for long periods of time, may become rigid or limp when held, may not mould to the parent when held, may not establish or maintain eye contact, and may not respond or interact socially. Autistic infants may be extremely irritable, may overreact to any type of stimulation, and may show early signs of feeding and sleep disturbances. The severity of unusual behaviors varies; in general, the more severe the behavior, the earlier the child will likely be diagnosed.

Most researchers and clinicians agree that symptoms are clearly evident by 24 to 30 months of age. For a diagnosis of autism, the disturbances must be evident by delays or abnormal functioning prior to age 3. By this time, the child's apparent hearing deficits, language delays, and abnormal social interaction suggest developmental problems. This often prompts referral for speech and hearing assessment. Normal hearing and the absence of physical speech deficits suggest the possibility of other disorders, including autism. However, despite the prevalence of early symptoms, some children with autism remain undiagnosed until they are of school age.

Behavioral Symptoms

Ornitz and Ritvo [1976] divide the common behavioral symptoms of autism into five major categories.

Disturbances of Perception

People with autism may be either hyperresponsive to sensory stimuli, or they may not respond at all. They may appear not to hear, see, or feel things. They may not respond to persons or objects in the environment. They may sustain bad falls, bumps, or bruises, and appear not to experience any discomfort. "Indifferent" and "remote" are adjectives often used to describe people with autism.

Conversely, they may be hypersensitive and may overreact to visual, auditory, and tactile stimuli, becoming easily agitated and distressed. Bright lights, harsh or loud sounds such as sirens or vacuum cleaners, physical contact with rough fabrics or other uncomfortable objects, and physical contact with other people may cause significant distress for people with autism. They might close their eyes or put their hands over their ears to ward off sights and sounds, and they may actively avoid physical contact.

Some persons with autism may seek out visual, auditory, and tactile stimulation. They may create noises and listen to them intently, visually explore minute details of objects for long periods of time, or rub objects of varying textures. Whirling, rocking, hand flapping, and head rolling appear to be attempts to generate vestibular and proprioceptive stimulation (sensory feedback from movements of the body).

All of the above patterns of behavior are thought to be the result of an underlying neurological dysfunction. Persons with autism are believed to be unable to process sensory stimuli appropriately. They lack the ability to interpret or correctly use information from visual and auditory sensory input; the senses of smell, touch, and taste seem to be preferred by persons with autism. This is different from the preferences of most children, who rely most on the senses of sight and hearing.

Disturbances in Rate of Development

The expected course of normal development is disrupted in children with autism, and these delays become more apparent as the child grows. The development of a child with autism is often characterized by spurts and plateaus, and the rates of development between the physical, cognitive, social, and emotional domains may be inconsistent. Children with autism have been noted to sit without assistance at an early age, but then fail to pull themselves to standing. Others may unexpectedly stand and walk without preparatory motor experimentation and practice.

In many children with autism, motor development and coordination may be normal, while they remain significantly delayed in cognitive, social, and emotional development. Approximately 75% of children with autism show generalized cognitive retardation, usually at the moderate level. However, the profile of cognitive skills is usually uneven, regardless of the general level of intelligence, and some children display some peculiar or exceptional cognitive abilities.

Disturbance in Social Development and Use of Objects

Persons with autism show characteristic disturbances in both their relationships with other people and in the way they use objects. Relationships with people are often characterized by failure to make eye contact; absence of social smiling; an aversion to physical contact with others; a tendency to relate to only parts of a person (i.e., a hand or an arm) rather than to the whole person; disinterest in social interaction, games, and activities with others; and delayed, absent, or overreactive anxiety in response to strangers.

It is common for persons with autism to play with toys and use other objects in a bizarre and inappropriate manner. This is different from the imaginative play typical of young children, who may ride a broom handle as if it were a horse, or create a tent under the dining room table. For example, a child with autism may turn a bicycle upside down and spin the wheels for long periods, yet never attempt to sit on or ride the bike. Or, the child may place a toy on the floor and repeatedly run around it in circles. Adults with autism may flick, twirl, spin, bang, or otherwise use objects in unusual ways. At other times, a person with autism may pay no attention to objects at all.

These inappropriate relationships with people and objects are thought to be symptoms of the more basic disturbance in perception. A person cannot relate appropriately to his environment, if he is not able to make sense of or integrate his perceptions into a consistent picture of reality. If a person does not understand what is happening around him, he cannot relate to his surroundings in normal ways. It is especially hard to be involved in social relationships, where the recognition and understanding of subtle social cues are necessary.

Disturbances of Speech and Language

Many persons with autism do not talk at all, while others develop some verbal communication ability. However, those who do learn language often display characteristic abnormalities in their language and speech patterns. Persons with autism often speak in a flat, toneless, mechanized manner. Voice inflections and verbal expressions of feeling are noticeably absent. Speech patterns often include echolalia and continuous repetition of selected words or phrases, as if the goal of speech were the production of rhythmic sounds, not interpersonal communication.

Persons with autism often interpret and associate speech concretely. For example, an 8-year-old boy with autism was given a candy bar. He replied, "Look at that bear." The phrase was meaningless when spoken in the middle of his living room in response to receiving a candy bar. However, his brother recalled that the last time the boy had been given a candy bar was at the zoo, near the bear cage. The child with autism had evidently associated the phrase "Look at that bear," to the receipt of a candy bar, rather than to the bear at the zoo.

Pronoun reversal is also common. Children with autism may refer to themselves as "you" and to other people as "I." This use of pronouns replicates the speech patterns used by other people; it is a concrete repetition of what is heard, rather than the utilization of pronouns in proper context.

Disturbances in Motility

Persons with autism are often described as having bizarre behaviors and peculiar, stereotyped actions. These may include atypical gross and fine motor activities, such as rocking, swaying, lunging, darting, lurching, toe walking, hand flapping, posturing, and twirling. Researchers concur that these behaviors are also related to an underlying central nervous system dysfunction. Some persons with autism also exhibit self-injurious behaviors.

Treatment and Prognosis

The prognosis for persons with autism is variable, although most persons with autism may be considered severely to profoundly developmentally disabled.

A small minority of children with autism have relatively normal motor development and use language in appropriate ways to communicate by the age of 5. These children appear to be less severely affected. They may often attend school and learn in a classroom setting, and they may be able to acquire some vocational skills. They typically remain shy, introverted, and passively social as adolescents and adults.

Approximately two-thirds of persons with autism are classified as mentally retarded or mentally ill (psychotic) as adults. These persons need care and supervision throughout their life. They display severe limitations in cognitive, social, and emotional functioning.

Autism cannot be cured, and there are few treatment interventions that can successfully minimize the effects of the disorder. While biological processes are believed to contribute to the disorder, these are not well understood, and there are no medical or drug treatments that can significantly modify the child's condition. Behavior modification strategies may be used to encourage the development of language or to help persons learn basic adaptive skills, but these have varying degrees of success.

Because persons with autism may be emotionally withdrawn, remote, and difficult to manage behaviorally, their families often need a great deal of support. Special programs for caregivers of autistic persons provide families with the skills and resources needed to manage chronic stress. Caregivers can often benefit from periods of respite care. Placement in a group home or other community-based living arrangement, where staff can share caregiving responsibility and support one another, may also be an appropriate alternative to family care for persons with autism.

Other Pervasive Developmental Disorders

The other conditions in the classification of pervasive developmental disorders can be differentiated from autistic disorder primarily in their age of onset and by some specific differences in their characteristics [American Psychiatric Association 1994]. These disorders appear to be much less common than autistic disorder.

Rett's syndrome has been diagnosed only in females, and its multiple deficits follow a period of normal development after birth. The pattern of developmental regression is highly distinctive, and the loss of skills is generally persistent and progressive. Children with Rett's syndrome have apparently normal psychomotor development for the first 5 months of life, and their head circumference at birth is within normal limits. Between the ages of 5 and 48 months, head growth decelerates, and there is a loss of previously acquired purposeful hand skills. The child often develops characteristic stereotyped hand movements that resemble hand wringing or hand washing. Interest in the social environment diminishes in the first few years after the onset of the disorder. Children with Rett's syndrome also have severe impairments in expressive and receptive language. Severe or profound mental retardation is typical, and various nonspecific neurological symptoms or signs may be noted, including increased frequency of EEG abnormalities and seizures.

In *childhood disintegrative disorders*, there is marked regression in multiple areas of functioning, but only after a period of at least two years of apparently normal development that includes age-appropriate verbal and nonverbal communication, social relationships, play, and adaptive behavior. At some time after two years, but before age 10, there is a clinically significant loss of previously acquired skills in several areas. These children eventually exhibit the social and communication deficits and behaviors typical of children with autism. Eventually, these children become severely mentally retarded, and nonspecific neurological symptoms may be noted, including an increase in EEG abnormalities and seizure disorders.

In *Asperger's syndrome*, children exhibit severe and sustained impairments in social interaction, as well as repetitive and restrictive patterns of behavior and activities, similar to that of children with autism. For example, children with Asperger's syndrome lack social or emotional reciprocity, and they show a marked impairment in the use of nonverbal behaviors, such as eye contact, facial expressions, or gestures, to regulate social interaction. They may inflexibly adhere to specific, nonfunctional routines or rituals. They may also exhibit a persistent preoccupation with parts of objects, or with stereotyped and restricted patterns of interest that are abnormal either in focus or in intensity. However, Asperger's syndrome differs from autism in that the children usually exhibit no significant delays in language, in cognitive development, in the development of age-appropriate self-help skills, or in adaptive behavior (other than social interaction). Children with Asperger's syndrome also display normal curiosity about the environment. There may be some delay in motor development, and motor clumsiness may be evident.

The general category of "pervasive developmental disorder not otherwise specified" is used when the presentation of the child's disorder does not meet the specific criteria for the other pervasive developmental disorders. This category includes "atypical autism" because of late age at onset, unusual symptoms, mild symptoms, or all of the above [American Psychiatric Association 1994].

ATTENTION-DEFICIT/ HYPERACTIVITY DISORDER AND LEARNING DISABILITIES

Attention-deficit/hyperactivity disorder (ADHD) is a relatively common condition in children. It is estimated that 3 to 5% of school-age children have the disorder. It is more prevalent in males than females, with ratios of males to females ranging from 4:1 to 9:1. ADHD is believed to be the result of an underlying neurologic disorder; however, the cause and exact nature of the condition have not been determined. It is more prevalent in certain families, suggesting possible genetic determinants.

ADHD is characterized primarily by the child's difficulty in maintaining attention and concentration. This inability to maintain sustained mental effort leads to considerable difficulty adjusting in academic, occupational, and social situations.

While most individuals with ADHD have symptoms of both inattention and hyperactivity-impulsivity, there are some persons in whom one pattern is more predominant than the other. The signs and symptoms of the disorder also vary with the child's age and developmental level.

The primary symptoms of ADHD, inattention, hyperactivity, and impulsivity, are described below [American Psychiatric Association 1994].

The signs of *inattention* may include the following:

- Individual has difficulty with tasks that require sustained mental effort or close attention, is unable to persist with tasks until completion, and frequently shifts from one uncompleted activity to another.

- Tasks that require sustained mental effort are experienced as unpleasant and markedly aversive; individuals typically avoid or have a strong dislike for such activities.

- Work is messy and is performed carelessly, without considered thought; careless mistakes are often made in school work and other tasks.

- Individual often fails to follow through on requests or instructions.

- Individual has difficulty organizing tasks and activities; work habits are often disorganized; and materials needed for the task are scattered, lost, or carelessly handled and damaged.

- Individual is easily distracted by irrelevant stimuli and frequently interrupts ongoing tasks to attend to trivial noises or events that are easily ignored by others.

- Individual is "forgetful" in daily activities, misses appointments, forgets to bring things.

- In social situations, individual may appear not to listen to others, may not stay focused on the interaction, fails to follow details or rules of a situation, and exhibits frequent shifts in conversation.

The signs of *hyperactivity* in children often include the following:

- Individual fidgets continuously, squirms, bounces or rocks; does not remain seated when expected to do so;

- Individual runs, jumps, or climbs excessively in situations where it is inappropriate;

- Individual has difficulty sitting still to play quietly or engage in sedentary leisure activities;

- Individual appears to be always "on the go" or "driven by a motor";

- Individual fidgets with objects, taps hands, shakes feet or legs excessively; and

- Individual talks excessively, makes excessive noise during quiet activities.

Impulsivity in behavior is another common symptom of ADHD. Indicators include the following:

- Children may exhibit considerable impatience, have difficulty in delaying responses, blurt out answers before questions have been completed, make comments out of turn, initiate conversations at inappropriate times, and have difficulty waiting for their turn.

- Children often interrupt or intrude on others, grab objects from others, touch things they are not supposed to touch, and clown around. Impulsivity may lead to accidents and engaging in potentially dangerous activities without considering the possible consequences.

In adolescents and adults, the behavioral symptoms of hyperactivity may subside and are often replaced by feelings of restlessness, fidgetiness, or an inner feeling of jitteriness and discomfort in situations that require sedentary activity or sustained attention. Difficulty in sustained attention may persist into adulthood.

ADHD may often present as soon as a child learns to walk or move around independently. However, it is important that toddlers and preschoolers not be prematurely diagnosed with ADHD, since overactivity is a hallmark of this developmental stage, and many excessively active toddlers and preschoolers do not exhibit either inattention or hyperactivity during the school years. In general, ADHD is first diagnosed during elementary school years, when school adjustment is compromised.

It is also important not to automatically diagnose ADHD whenever a child exhibits excessive activity or inattention. This is particularly true in populations of maltreated children, or children who have experienced traumatic separations. Inattention and overactivity, particularly in a school setting, are common symptoms of anxiety in children, and may reflect a pressing preoccupation with other worries and concerns. Inattention is also common when children are inappropriately placed in academic settings, either from boredom because they are not sufficiently challenged, or in response to feeling overwhelmed because the classroom demands exceed their intellectual ability. Children from chaotic and disorganized home environments may also exhibit disorganized and chaotic behavior, and may not be able to sustain goal-directed behavior. Finally, some individuals may resist work or school tasks that require self-application because they are unwilling to conform to others' demands. Most children with ADHD fail to conform to expectations because they cannot—not because they don't want to. However, after years of negative responses to their disruptive behaviors, many children and youths with ADHD develop negative and oppositional attitudes about school, work, and conforming to social expectations.

Early identification, proper diagnosis, and appropriate intervention are critical in helping children with ADHD. For many children, and for many adults who have had ADHD since childhood, medication can significantly reduce hyperactivity, counteract feelings of restlessness, and make it easier to focus and sustain attention. Ritalin, or methylphenidate hydrochloride, is a mild central nervous system stimulant that appears to have a paradoxical, calming effect in many persons with ADHD. Ritalin is the most frequently used drug to treat ADHD. However, in some cases it may exacerbate rather than reduce symptoms. (Many parents have also found their children to be unusually sensitive to many common chemicals in foods, and restricting their children's intake of preservatives, excessive sugar, and other chemicals also helps to lessen their hyperactive behavior.)

Treatment must include an appropriate educational placement and, when appropriate, supportive counseling to help families understand the disorder and to learn appropriate responses. Parents or caregivers must first understand that their child's behavior is not under the child's control, and that punishment for hyperactive behaviors and inattention will often exacerbate the child's emotional distress. Parents must help the child set realistic and achievable expectations (for example, helping the child focus and concentrate for five minutes at a stretch rather than 25) and reward the child for small, but successful, efforts at self-control and attentiveness.

There are a number of behavioral strategies that parents and caregivers can implement to help children with ADHD to better learn and adapt to their environments. Parents can reduce environmental distractions, including lights, objects, and noise when the child is trying to attend to tasks. Parents can direct children to take frequent, but controlled breaks, while working at a task. They can help the child to expend excessive energy in nonharmful ways, such as running outside rather than in the house, or throwing a sponge ball rather than a softball. Parents should intervene early in misbehavior, redirect the child whenever possible, and ignore less problematic hyperactive or impulsive behaviors. Positive rewards for small achievements are necessary to promote the development of self-esteem and self-confidence.

Learning Disabilities

The term "learning disabilities" is commonly used to describe a variety of conditions characterized primarily by an inability to take in, process, express, and/or retain sensory information. Learning disabilities can include impairment in one or more aspects of a broad range of cognitive functioning, including attention, memory, visual perception, receptive language, expressive language, motor output, and higher order conceptualization.

The most common type of learning disability is known as dyslexia, which derives from the combination of *dys* meaning "hard or difficult," and *lexia*, from the Greek *lexikos*, meaning "pertaining to words." Difficulty with words and letters is called dyslexia, which can manifest itself in speaking, reading, or writing.

Many children with learning disabilities also exhibit behavior disorders, including disruptive behavior, hyperactivity, and difficulties in social and emotional interaction. Thain et al. [1980] believe that the combination of learning and behavior disorders represents a syndrome that includes these primary symptoms. Other theorists suggest that the associated emotional and behavioral disorders are secondary and may be a consequence of the primary problem of difficulty in learning.

It is generally agreed that learning disabilities have their roots in brain dysfunction; however, theorists vary widely in their explanations of how this occurs. Some clearly object to the use of such terms as brain damage or minimal brain dysfunction, as these connote brain pathology. Alternative explanations for learning disorders can be made in terms of the existence of maturational or developmental lags, perhaps caused by failure to establish unilateral brain superiority with a definite pattern of hemispheric dominance, and of other constitutional origins, probably genetically determined, and unlikely to be the product of damage to the brain at birth [Levine 1980].

Considering the foregoing, it is not surprising that much confusion exists in diagnosis and intervention for the many conditions included under the rubric of learning disorders.

Learning disorders occur in boys approximately 5 to 9 times as often as in girls. Estimates of the numbers of school children affected are as high as 10%. Learning disabilities should be differentiated from mental retardation. Children with learning disabilities are generally impaired in only a few specific cognitive or perceptual skill areas, while mentally retarded children typically show comparable degrees of delay across all developmental areas. Special education programs that provide alternative means of learning can help children with learning disabilities develop to their full capacity, while minimizing the effects of the learning disability. Early identification and intervention are critical to prevent subsequent social and emotional problems.

PRENATAL EXPOSURE TO ALCOHOL AND OTHER DRUGS

Fetal Alcohol Syndrome (FAS) and Fetal Alcohol Effects (FAE)

In 1973, Jones and Smith described a distinct pattern of physical abnormalities and central nervous system dysfunction in 11 children whose mothers were chronic alcoholics [Jones & Smith 1973]. Fetal alcohol syndrome (FAS) is now recognized as one of the most frequent syndromes associated with impaired cognitive functioning. A less severe pattern of malformation that primarily affects behavior has been called fetal alcohol effects (FAE) [Caruso & ten Bensel 1993; Coles 1993]. The widespread use of alcohol makes it the most common major teratogen (environmental insult) to which a fetus can be exposed.

Incidence of FAS is estimated at 1 to 3 per 1,000 live births. Studies estimate that 10 to 20% of mild mental retardation and low-normal cognitive functioning are the result of prenatal exposure to excessive alcohol [Smith 1982]. Among alcoholic women who drink during pregnancy, approximately 35 to 40% of their infants will have fetal alcohol syndrome, and up to 3 times as many will have fetal alcohol effects.

Following are the primary symptoms of fetal alcohol syndrome:

- Prenatal and postnatal growth deficiency (failure to grow). FAS children tend to be lower in birth weight and demonstrate generalized growth retardation. Average is below the fifth percentile for age.

- Typical facial features include flattened midface; epicanthal folds on the eyes; short, upturned nose; thin upper lip.

- An average I.Q. of about 68 to 70, which falls within the mild range of mental retardation.

- Irritability in infancy, hyperactivity and other emotional and behavior disorders throughout childhood, including attention deficit disorder (ADD), with hyperactivity (ADHD), and poor social judgment.

- Mild to moderate degrees of microcephaly. (Microcephaly is small head circumference. It is usually associated with varying degrees of mental retardation and abnormal brain development.)

- Dysfunction in fine motor control, such as weak grasp, poor eye-hand coordination, and tremulousness.

Fetal alcohol effects (FAE) is generally the diagnosis when there are few physical deformities and the child does not meet the criteria for FAS. However, these children do manifest many of the behavioral and central nervous system disturbances, such as attention deficit disorder (ADD), with hyperactivity (ADHD), poor social judgment, and delayed learning. These children also have a subnormal I.Q., which helps to differentiate them from children with ADD or ADHD from other causes [Caruso & ten Bensel 1993].

Research suggests that the extent of disability is highly correlated with the amount of prenatal exposure to alcohol. Low infant birth weight has been associated with maternal ingestion of as few as two drinks per day. With four to six drinks per day, additional clinical symptoms become more evident. Heavy maternal alcohol consumption is generally defined as five or more drinks per day. The most severe effects of FAS were seen in children born to alcoholic women whose average intake was eight to 10 drinks per day or more.

It is sometimes difficult to isolate the effects of alcohol on development from the effects of other factors. Mothers of FAS children frequently have no prenatal care and take other drugs, such as cocaine and/or marijuana. Many studies report that FAS/FAE children seldom remain with their birth mothers; a high percentage are placed in foster care, relatives' homes, or are adopted [Caruso & ten Bensel 1993]. In one study, many FAS infants were reportedly taken from their alcoholic mothers because of constant neglect or the risk of severe deprivation; some were institutionalized because of acute life-threatening circumstances [Spohr et al. 1993]. These factors would be likely to exacerbate the developmental problems resulting from prenatal alcohol exposure.

Longitudinal and follow-up studies of children with fetal alcohol syndrome suggest that as these children grow, the characteristic physical features and minor physical abnormalities diminish or disappear, and there is improvement in internal organ functions, growth patterns, and skeletal abnormalities. However, the prognosis for cognitive and emotional development is not as good. Most children remained mentally retarded. In addition, several psychological disorders were common, including conduct disorders, hyperkinetic and attention deficit disorders, emotional disorders, speech disorders, and problems in social relationships. In general, the greater the prenatal exposure to alcohol, the greater the severity and duration of intellectual and emotional impairment [Steinhausen et al. 1993; Spohr et al. 1973].

Recommended interventions include the following:

- Preventive education and counseling to pregnant women regarding the risks to their babies from ingesting alcohol during pregnancy. It is important to note that the most susceptible period in embryonic development to alcohol abuse is from day nine to day 41—often before the mother is even aware she is pregnant [Caruso & ten Bensel 1993]. This does not suggest, however, that drinking later in pregnancy is safe.

- Referral of pregnant women who abuse alcohol to medical services and alcoholism programs to help them reduce or eliminate alcohol consumption during pregnancy.

- Developmental assessment of children thought to have been exposed prenatally to alcohol.

- Referral of affected children to infant stimulation, early intervention, and special education programs. Children with FAS must be assessed to determine the degree of developmental delay or mental retardation. Educational programs should be planned accordingly.

- Training parents or caregivers to plan and implement activities that will address developmental delays and emotional problems.

- Appropriate educational programming. Vocational programs have been found to be more successful than traditional school programs in teaching youth with FAS useful living and working skills [Caruso & ten Bensel 1993]. However, case planning for each child should follow from individual assessment.

Prenatal Exposure to Drugs

The research is consistent in its reporting of the effects of fetal exposure to drugs, including crack cocaine, on prenatal and postnatal child development. Studies have repeatedly confirmed that prenatal drug exposure has significant negative effects on early infant growth and development.

In a review of several research studies published from 1988 to 1994, there were several outcomes consistently associated with prenatal fetal exposure to crack and cocaine, either alone or in combination with other drugs, such as heroin or methadone [Anday et al. 1989; Azuma et al. 1993; Chasnoff et al. 1989a, 1989b, 1989c; Cherukuri et al. 1988; Ross Laboratories 1989; Dobercza et al. 1988; Fulroth et al. 1989; Griffith et al. 1994; Hadeed & Siegel 1989; Howard et al. 1989; Kaye et al. 1989; Little et al. 1989; MacGregor 1987; Scherling 1994; Zuckerman et al. 1989].

Cocaine-exposed infants typically had lower birth weight and growth retardation. The weight, length, and head circumference growth curves for these infants were typically below the 25th percentile. Birth weight of cocaine exposed infants averaged 423 grams less than controls. Infants exposed to cocaine also had an increased risk of preterm delivery, with gestation averaging 37 weeks rather than the typical 39 to 40 weeks.

Infants exposed to cocaine had a smaller head circumference. Seventeen percent of infants in one study and 21.4% in another study were microcephalic. A third study indicated that these infants were 2.8 times as likely to have a head circumference that was below the 10th percentile. Small head size appeared to persist at least through age 2.

Infants exposed to cocaine had a higher rate of perinatal complications (immediately before, during, or immediately after birth.) Complications included mild abnormal neurobehavioral symptoms; increased meconium (the presence of bowel excretions in the amniotic fluid, which increases the risk of infection); tachycardia and other heart abnormalities; and impairment of orientation and motor activity. A high percentage of cocaine-exposed children had central nervous system irritability and abnormal EEGs during the first week. The brain wave patterns did appear to revert to normal after several months.

Crack was noted to be worse than cocaine with respect to adverse neurological signs and low birth weights. Also, mothers who used more than one drug placed their infants at considerably higher risk than did single drug users. For instance, simultaneous use of crack cocaine and heroin or crack cocaine and methadone appeared to greatly increase the risks of negative developmental consequences. These infants were also more likely to need treatment for symptoms of withdrawal at birth.

Initial studies conclude that the effects of cocaine exposure persist into the toddler and early preschool years, with resulting problems in attention, cognitive organization, affect and emotion, socialization, and play.

Research suggests that children exposed to crack are often difficult to care for from birth. They are likely to be born prematurely, with all the risks normally associated with premature birth. They may be irritable or extremely lethargic. They often have poor sucking ability that hinders feeding, and alternative feeding methods or schedules may be required. Their sleep patterns may also be irregular. These infants also often demonstrate poor or insecure attachment.

Chasnoff et al. [1989a; 1989c] studied 2- and 3-year-olds who had been prenatally exposed to crack. Their intelligence on standardized I.Q. tests was found to be generally comparable to the intelligence of children from similar environments, but who had not been exposed to drugs. However, the ability of the cocaine-exposed children to concentrate was impaired. They were distractible and easily frustrated, they had difficulty organizing and responding in planned ways to their environments, and they had considerable difficulty playing in unstructured settings. They appeared to be unable to organize their own play activities.

Howard et al. [1989] compared 18 toddlers who had been exposed to cocaine prenatally with a control group of 18 premature children who had not been exposed to drugs. All children were from similar socioeconomic environments. In the study, although the children exposed to cocaine performed within the normal range on developmental assessments, their developmental scores were significantly lower overall than those of children not exposed to drugs. The cocaine-exposed children also performed better in the highly structured environment of the developmental assessment than they did in free play situations; they appeared to have difficulty in structuring and organizing their own activities. The toddlers exposed to cocaine did not play appropriately with toys; they scattered and batted at them and manipulated them without apparent goal or purpose. They also engaged in significantly less representational play, fantasy play, or curious exploration. They demonstrated little initiative; many would play only if an adult initiated the activity. They had trouble playing with and talking with other children.

The drug-exposed children also showed little emotion and were described as "joyless" and "dispassionate." They did not show strong feelings of pleasure, anger, or distress in appropriate situations; they appeared to be withdrawn, apathetic, and had flat affect. They demonstrated insecure attachment characterized by disorganization, rather than avoidance or ambivalence. They showed minimal anxiety and separation distress when left by their caregivers. Their attention span was significantly less than that of nonexposed children. Because of the demonstrated link between representational play and the development of language, the investigators anticipated problems in the children's later language development.

Many studies have also suggested that the quality of the children's home environments was often adversely affected by ongoing parental drug abuse. Children in substance abusing families typically experience neglect, physical abuse, disorganization, and inconsistent care. Chronic drug use distorts a parent's thoughts and perceptions and affects memory and attention. Some physicians suspect that some children may also be further injured by breathing the crack-filled smoke in their homes.

In some respects, drug-exposed children reared by caregivers addicted to crack cocaine may be at significantly higher risk of long-term developmental harm than are drug-exposed children who are reared in drug-free environments. This is related to the often serious neglect and abuse experienced by children of addicted parents. The drug addiction is often so strong that it overwhelms all other considerations of either maternal health or child well-being. Children of addicted parents are often neither fed nor nurtured. They are often abandoned or are left in the care of unreliable caregivers. They may be exposed to crime, drug dealing, and childhood prostitution. Family financial resources are often directed toward maintaining the addiction, rather than providing healthful care for the child [MacGregor, et al. 1987; Scherling 1994; Howard et al. 1989; Zuckerman et al. 1989].

Intensive interventions are necessary if children exposed to drugs are to be successfully maintained with their parents without risk of serious developmental problems. The following strategies are recommended:

- Prevention is the best intervention. Pregnant women should always be counseled regarding the risks to their offspring of any drug use. Referral of mothers early in their pregnancies to medical services and substance abuse programs is essential.

- Thorough medical, developmental, and psychological assessments should be performed when children are believed to have been prenatally exposed to drugs to identify any health or developmental problems.

- Many children will benefit from infant stimulation, early intervention, and special education programs. They may require highly structured and consistent school environments. Low pupil-teacher ratios in preschool settings can provide the one-to-one attention that is often necessary to help the children acquire social and play skills.

- Parents and other caregivers should be trained to provide activities that promote healthy development, and can mitigate the negative effects of drug exposure. The home environment should be highly structured and consistent. Parents will probably need training in methods to manage the children's behavior and to structure daily activities.

The continuing abuse of drugs by parents creates a high risk of abuse and neglect for their children [Besharov 1994]. Parents should routinely be referred to drug treatment programs. They often need intensive education in parenting skills as well, specifically in providing nurturance and structure for their children. Several studies reviewed by Chavkin et al. [1993] suggest that maternal drug users consistently experienced feelings of shame, guilt, and failure for providing inadequately for their children or for exposing them to drug-dominated environments. Some mothers are, therefore, receptive to therapy designed to help them build relationships with, and care for, their children. Chavkin et al. also report that concern for their children's well-being has motivated many addicted mothers to enter drug treatment. Treatment must, however, be broad-based, and address the complex social, environmental, and emotional contributors to drug use.

We do not yet have longitudinal studies of sufficient scope to determine the long-term developmental implications for children exposed to intrauterine cocaine. Many researchers stress the difficulty in distinguishing the direct effects of prenatal drug exposure on child development from the effects of other maternal and environmental factors, including abuse and neglect resulting from parental polydrug use and addiction. Early data suggest that, while a structured and stimulating home environment can foster secure attachment and mitigate the impact of drug exposure on development, it does not entirely eliminate the long-term negative effects. Further study is necessary to determine the long-range effects of prenatal exposure to crack and cocaine on children's development.

SERVICES FOR CHILDREN WITH DEVELOPMENTAL DISABILITIES AND THEIR FAMILIES

In the early 1970s, strong political and legislative advocacy resulted in a redefinition of appropriate services for persons with developmental disabilities. Historically, many people with mental retardation and other disabilities were cared for in institutions. Some were placed at birth and others in later childhood or early adulthood, when their care became too challenging for their families. Parents who preferred to raise their children at home often could not. Many parents lacked the skills and resources to meet their children's special needs, and community-based supportive services were rare or nonexistent. For many years, the prevailing view among both professionals and lay persons was that institutionalization was in the best interests of persons with disabilities, as well as their families. In fact, one of the original functions of institutions was "to relieve the family of the perceived burden of caring for a child who had mental retardation" [Wikler 1986].

The broader civil rights movement of the 1960s and 1970s prompted a reexamination of society's treatment of persons with disabilities. Advocates were successful in gaining passage of federal legislation that assured people with disabilities the right to grow, be educated, live, and work in typical family and community environments. This legislation also required "reasonable accommodation" to enable persons with disabilities to have access to and function more independently in those environments. A proliferation of structural changes resulted, including the installation of wheelchair ramps at curbs and in buildings; installation of motorized lifts on buses; increased public transportation options; installation of electronic door openers; mounting telephones and drinking fountains within easy reach; posting signs and instruction panels in braille; and widespread availability of accessible bathrooms, hotel rooms, and apartments. The legislation also generated federal funding to support special education, as well as health-related, employment, and family support services, and created fiscal sanctions for noncompliance.

One of the most important outcomes of the advocacy movement was deinstitutionalization. Large congregate care institutions, once the placement of choice for persons with disabilities, were found, at best, to be overly restrictive, unnecessarily segregating, and incapable of supporting healthy development. At worst, these institutions were destructive and dehumanizing environments that frequently failed to meet even the most basic of human needs. Many persons with disabilities were subsequently discharged from institutions into community-based living environments, and many of the institutions were permanently closed. Unfortunately, many communities lack the array of supportive services needed by many persons with developmental disabilities.

These changes have had a profound impact on the nature of services to children with developmental disabilities and their families. The goal for all children with disabilities is to provide a healthy, developmentally stimulating environment in a family setting whenever possible, with community-based supportive services to meet the child's special needs. This goal is entirely consistent with the goals and premises of a family-centered approach to services for abused and neglected children. To achieve this goal, we must understand the family's service needs, and we must develop and provide a wide array of developmental, therapeutic, and supportive services. Since children with disabilities have the same fundamental needs as all children, we can serve them effectively within the framework of other family-centered services, with linkage to special services as needed. We must also understand the unique stresses and needs experienced by families parenting children with developmental disabilities, and we must address these special needs as well.

Crisis Intervention Theory

Crisis intervention theory is particularly useful in understanding a family's response to a child with a disability and in assessing their strengths and service needs [Parad & Caplan 1965; Wikler 1986; Dyson 1991; Beckman 1983].

Crisis intervention theory is based upon the interaction of three dynamics that together cause crisis:

- The nature and severity of the stress experienced by a family;

- The family's coping strategies, including the supports and resources available to them; and

- The family members' perceptions of their situation.

Stress

McCubbin and Patterson [1983] describe a stressor as a "life event or transition impacting upon the family unit which produces, or has the potential of producing, change in the family social system." Stress is a state that arises when there is an imbalance between a demand for change and a person's inherent resources to cope with that change. The presence of a child with a developmental disability should be considered a potential stress factor for nearly all families. At times, the stresses associated with caregiving may become severe enough to precipitate a family crisis. Such crises may place a child at higher risk of abuse or neglect [Petr & Barney 1993].

Several factors have been shown to correlate with increased stress in families of children with developmental disabilities. It must be remembered that a stressful event does not, by itself, determine the degree of psychological distress experienced by family members. The relative weight of any stressor must be determined within a context that also considers whether the family has sufficient resources and supports to cope with the stressor and the family's perception of the meaning of the stressful event, including their perception of its effects on family life. The responses of different families to comparable events will vary considerably. Thus, while the factors listed below may generally increase the likelihood of family distress, each family's response must be evaluated individually.

- *The degree and severity of the child's disability.* A chronic (long-term) or severe condition tends to result in more stress than a condition that is correctable or of less severity. In general, the more the child's disability limits the child's functioning and interferes with normal growth and development, the greater the potential for family distress.

- *The child's life expectancy.* Family stress can be considerably greater when a condition, such as cystic fibrosis or internal organ deformities, is life-threatening or is likely to reduce a child's life expectancy. The stress is especially acute if the quality of the parents' care can influence the child's survival.

- *The degree of specialized care required.* Some disabling conditions require considerable special care, often creating excessive demands on the caregiver. Feeding, bathing, toileting, and transporting a child may be time-consuming and difficult tasks for family members and may disrupt normal family routines and activities. Children with disabilities may be more dependent upon other people for a long period of time, and some persons with disabilities require nursing care for life. This can place additional stress on the family.

- *Visibility.* A condition that is highly visible or results in an unusual physical appearance often evokes unpleasant reactions from other people. Parents of children with disabilities are regularly confronted with negative stereotypic attitudes about their children and inappropriate behavior from strangers. Wikler [1986] suggests that the stigma associated with mental retardation in our society is a constant stress factor for families throughout the child's life, particularly when friends and extended family members display negative attitudes toward and about the child.

- *The child's temperament and responsiveness.* Research has suggested that family stress may be related to the child's temperament and particularly to the child's ability to give and receive affection. As would be expected, children who were more socially responsive, affectionate, and less demanding were rated less stressful by their caregivers than children who were difficult to satisfy, and who were socially nonresponsive and unable to reciprocate affection [Beckman 1983; Wikler 1986].

- *The presence of stressors unrelated to the child's condition.* The total amount of life stress experienced by a family, including stresses not directly related to the child's disability, can contribute to the development of crisis. A family with limited income or multiple other problems may experience the effects of a child's developmental disability with more intensity than a family that has few other sources of stress.

Coping

Families have varying capacities to cope with stress. Families that have a variety of coping skills and strategies can generally mitigate stress, maintain stability, and prevent crisis. Families with limited coping capacity are much more likely to experience a stressful event as a psychological crisis.

Several factors can affect a family's ability to cope with stress. First, families with considerable skill in constructive planning and problem solving are generally less vulnerable to stress and more likely to manage their situation effectively. A family with a history of successful management of stress or illness may be more likely to respond with more confidence, as they can draw upon a repertoire of effective coping skills. Conversely, families whose coping abilities are limited, or who are already overtaxed from other problems, are more vulnerable to the effects of even minor stresses. The unusual needs of a child with a disability can promote crisis in these families.

The availability of emotional support and access to community resources are significant assets in managing stress. Conversely, the absence of such resources and supports can greatly exacerbate stress. Wikler [1986] reports several coping strategies that are correlated with decreased stress in families that have children with disabilities. These include the ability to organize formal support networks, such as parent associations; regular contact with a supportive kinship network; frequent church contact and a strong personal belief system; and a satisfying marital relationship prior to the birth of the child. Unfortunately, social isolation is a frequent occurrence in families of children with mental retardation and other disabilities. These families have been found to have a diminished circle of acquaintances, they belong to fewer organizations, they share fewer leisure time activities, and they lack vacation and respite time [Wikler 1986].

Perception of the Situation

The family's perception of their situation also influences the degree of distress experienced by the family. Rapoport [1965] contends that stresses are generally perceived in one of three characteristic ways and that this perception affects the emotional response to the stressor. Stress can be perceived as a threat, with resulting fear and anxiety; it can be perceived as a loss, with resulting grief and depression; or it can be perceived as a challenge, with increased productive coping responses.

A child with a disability may be perceived as a threat to the family in many ways. Normal family routines may be permanently disrupted. Parents may have to quit jobs to care for their child, resulting in lowered family income. Relationships between spouses, siblings, and with extended family members may become strained and conflicted. Siblings may feel threatened by the increased time and attention paid to the child with the disability. Parents may experience a threat to their own self-esteem and parenting competence, particularly if their parenting activities appear to have little positive effect on the child's health or development.

Most families also feel some degree of loss when they have a child with a disability. Losses may be concrete, such as the loss of time for a spouse, other children, or themselves; loss of financial stability; or loss of personal freedom and mobility for the parents. Losses may also be entirely psychological, such as parents grieving the loss of the child they might have had. Such feelings are normal in the early stages of adapting to a child with a disability, and an initial period of mourning is to be expected. Mourning beyond the initial period, however, is commonly referred to as chronic sorrow. In families where this occurs, chronic depression may interfere with the family's ability to cope.

If stressors are perceived primarily as a challenge, families are more likely to be mobilized to respond with positive, goal-directed, problem-solving activity. This goal-oriented mobilization is often directed toward providing experiences that help the child develop to his or her potential, to provide experiences in which family members can interact with and enjoy one another, and to assure that the developmental and emotional needs of other family members are met. This is effective both in its positive effects for the child with a disability and in reducing the family's susceptibility to crisis.

Wikler [1986] reports congruence in the literature on the effects of several common parental perceptions on parental stress. First, mothers appear to perceive their mentally retarded child as more of a hardship in direct proportion to their child's level of incapacitation and helplessness. Similarly, mothers' ability and enthusiasm for caregiving are adversely affected when the mothers perceive their children as unaffectionate and undemonstrative. Lower I.Q. levels of the child are related to increased stress and more frequent placement. Parents' social values, social standing, and socioeconomic class also can affect the ways in which they perceive mental retardation. In general, parents with higher levels of education tend to perceive mental retardation as more of a "tragedy." Wikler suggests that the "impact of the child's retardation may be triggered less by the child's capacity as measured on an absolute scale than by the discrepancy between the *actual* performance and the *expected* performance." Fathers reportedly have increased difficulty coping with mental retardation when the child is male; their perception seems to be related to concerns about the eventual performance of their sons in roles outside of the home. Wikler also reports that while parents generally appear to have accurate perceptions of their child's capabilities, there are "some dramatic exceptions."

A parent's perception of the impact a child with a disability has on the family may also be distorted. For example, a mother who must expend considerable effort caring for a child with special needs may feel that doing so is damaging to her other children. She may feel both anxious and depressed. However, reality may be quite different from her perception of it. Her children may gain emotional gratification by helping her care for their sibling, they may receive considerable attention and affection from grandparents and extended family members, and they may not equate their mother's lack of time with a lack of love for them. When helped to examine the situation from a more accurate perspective, the mother may realize that, while her concern remains valid, the real effect is considerably less than imagined.

Many parents' unrealistic fears and concerns are exacerbated by widely held negative attitudes, stereotypes, and misconceptions about persons with developmental disabilities. Such attitudes as, "This is permanent. It will never be better," or "This is a terrible tragedy." "Persons with disabilities can never live normal lives ... function independently ... live in the community ... get around on their own ..." and others create hopelessness and despair. The truth is often far different than the stereotypes would suggest. With developmental services and supportive resources, and with the benefits of technology, many persons with disabilities can, and do, live in independent or semi-independent situations. They learn and grow. They develop self-help skills. They may work, either in the community or sheltered job settings. And they enjoy and benefit from typical family and community activities. Only a small percentage of persons with developmental disabilities require extensive, long-term nursing care.

Helping families achieve a realistic perception of their situation includes recognizing how their perceived fears and losses may increase their stress, recognizing and learning to trust their own strengths and internal resources, developing positively realistic expectations for their children's growth, and learning to view their situation as an achievable challenge, with potentially positive outcomes for themselves and their children.

Service Needs of Families of Children with Disabilities

Services for families of children with disabilities must address all three factors of the crisis equation: the reduction of situational and psychological stress, strengthening a family's ability to cope and to access supportive services and resources, and helping the family achieve a realistic perception of their situation.

The service needs of families with children who have developmental disabilities typically fall into several major categories.

When the child's condition has a medical or physiological component, *ongoing medical care, monitoring and supervision, and/or rehabilitation services* are necessary. The nature of the child's medical condition must be accurately assessed and continually reevaluated. Therapeutic interventions must be closely monitored. Families may need special medical equipment and medications. In some situations, the most appropriate specialized medical resources may only be available in a large hospital or other specialized clinic located far from the family's home.

The special needs of many children with disabilities can create serious *financial stresses* for their families. Even with health insurance, the costs of care and management can become immense. The family may have to incur child care costs, or one parent may have to quit work to care for the child. Additional money may be needed for rehabilitative and therapeutic equipment, such as wheelchairs, braces, hearing aids, feeding utensils, and hospital beds. Homes may need to be renovated for wheelchair access. Total costs often exceed a family's financial resources. Although financial assistance programs are available, many families will need help in locating and applying for financial help. Again, because these special services are not available in many communities, travel costs may increase.

When a child's disability precludes the child's involvement in typical childhood activities, *special education and recreation resources* may be needed to promote healthy development. Such activities will change as the child grows. In infants, developmental activities will be needed to master sensory and motor skills and to stimulate cognitive development. As the child reaches preschool and school age, opportunities to develop positive peer relationships and to acquire social and self-help skills become important. If the adolescent with a disability is to be emancipated to semi-supervised or semi-independent living, he or she must learn self-care and home management skills. Throughout the child's life, the child should be involved in activities that are pleasurable and that enhance self-esteem and accomplishment. Special service programs may include infant stimulation, structured preschool, individual skill development, recreational programs, group socialization programs, special educational experiences, and work-study programs. These should be carefully planned to meet the needs of each child, combining these with participation in as many typical family and community activities as possible.

Even when services are readily available, *managing* them is often a complicated process. Many families need a variety of services offered through multiple agencies, and locating and accessing the most appropriate services is typically time consuming and stressful. Most families are unfamiliar with service systems and rules of eligibility, and they may become overwhelmed with the discouraging routine of seemingly endless referrals. Once service needs are identified, careful planning and coordination are essential to prevent the frustration associated with service gaps and overlaps, agency-hopping, and dead ends. Having a relationship with a primary caseworker who provides case management, advocacy, and interagency coordination can significantly reduce the family's stress.

Respite care is an essential service for many families. Respite care refers to child care provided by someone other than the parents or primary caregiver, allowing the family a period of relief from the stresses associated with the care of the child. The child may be placed temporarily in a substitute-care family or a formal child care facility. In-home child care services can also be provided. The respite period may be a few hours to several days in length. Extended respite allows family members to take vacations, gives parents time to themselves, and enables parents to give special attention to their other children. Respite care helps to avert crisis by intermittently relieving tension, reducing stress, and allowing families to rebuild their strengths.

Most parents will need *specialized training* to learn how to meet their child's special needs. This may include using special equipment to manage medical conditions, techniques to feed their child, or strategies to enhance their child's mobility. Formal therapeutic programming often must be maintained by parents at home through physical exercises or other types of programmed stimulation. Parents must also recognize warning signs of medical problems, and they must learn to manage unusual behaviors.

Finally, *family responses* to the presence of a child with a disability vary. In some families, members develop increased strength and cohesion. In others, there is a painful disruption of family relationships, high levels of grief and anxiety, and an inability to function effectively. Some families will require considerable supportive and therapeutic counseling to help them deal with their feelings and to understand and resolve the resulting problems. Other families manage well from day to day but may need supportive intervention when confronted with new problems and challenges as the child grows. The help of a knowledgeable counselor, the opportunity to resolve issues that interfere with family interaction, and the opportunity to participate in support groups with other parents can reduce stress and strengthen family integrity.

The Role of Child Welfare Agencies

Child welfare agencies regularly serve a large number of children with developmental disabilities. Most of these children enter the child welfare system as a result of abuse or neglect, or because they need temporary or permanent care. Because developmental disabilities have typically been perceived as secondary to the primary presenting problems of abuse and neglect, services for children with disabilities have not always been formally integrated into child welfare programs. When available, these services may be poorly planned or inconsistently applied, and delivery often depends upon the ingenuity and determination of the individual worker or agency. If we are to maintain children with disabilities in family and community settings, we must advocate for and deliver supportive, developmental, and therapeutic services to these children and their biological, foster, and adoptive families.

Services

Many regular child welfare services are appropriate for children with disabilities and their families, and some could routinely be made available with little or no program modification. Others could be expanded with few additional resources and could be offered as a regular component of child welfare interventions. In addition, establishing formal linkages and service agreements with other community agencies and service providers can greatly expand the type and scope of services child welfare agencies can offer to the families and children they serve.

Early Screening and Identification

The preventable nature of many developmental disabilities and the importance of early intervention have been previously discussed. Successful early intervention depends upon the existence of systems for regular screening of high-risk children and the prompt identification of disabling conditions.

Many children with disabilities are first diagnosed in the medical system because of obvious physical problems. However, other disabilities have no immediately apparent symptoms, and a child's condition may remain undiagnosed for months to years. Most families will not recognize developmental delays or understand their potential significance unless the delays are pronounced. Of course, failure to properly identify developmental disabilities makes it impossible to provide the early intervention services that promote healthy development and mitigate long-term negative effects. The following disabilities are often not properly recognized or diagnosed:

- *Absence seizures.* These may be infrequent enough that they do not appear during medical examination. When they are witnessed by parents, teachers, or other caregivers, they are often mistaken for daydreaming or inattention.

- *Cerebral palsy.* Mild involvement may not be evident at birth. The symptoms manifest themselves as delayed or abnormal motor development as the child grows. Some of these children may not receive routine medical check-ups, and their parents may not recognize the early signs of the condition. Many children with mild or moderate cerebral palsy are not properly diagnosed until they are in school.

- *Mild mental retardation.* While there is usually some evidence of early developmental delay, most children with mild mental retardation are not diagnosed until they begin school and demonstrate difficulty learning in an academic setting. Their delays become more pronounced as they get older.

- *Autism.* Many early cases are misdiagnosed as hearing problems or simply identified as emotional and behavioral dysfunctions of unknown origin.

- *Learning disabilities.* Learning disabilities are generally first diagnosed in school. Often, the school staff may think that the child is mentally retarded, and/or that he exhibits behavior problems.

- *Psychomotor epilepsy.* The symptoms of psychomotor epilepsy include severe behavioral and verbal outbursts that are often misdiagnosed as emotional disturbance or conduct disorders. Many children are punished for their behavior, not treated.

- *Attention-deficit/hyperactive disorder.* These children may be considered willfully overactive and oppositional and are often diagnosed with behavior and emotional problems. Identification of the disorder often occurs after the child begins school and has difficulty attending to academic tasks. However, some mild to moderate cases remain undiagnosed.

Child welfare workers have regular and frequent contact with a population of children at high risk of developmental disabilities. Many of these children do not receive regular or adequate medical care and assessment. Until they reach the age of mandatory public school attendance, the child welfare caseworker may be the only social service professional to have contact with them. Yet, many child welfare workers have no training in developmental disabilities, do not know how to recognize disabilities in children, and remain unaware of the importance of early identification and intervention. A minimum of training and education can adequately prepare most child welfare staff to recognize many disabilities and provide effective interventions.

To increase its effectiveness in the identification of developmental disabilities, an agency can develop a formal comprehensive screening and assessment process. Staff can regularly conduct general screening for developmental delays in children on their caseloads, either by comparing children's development against age-expected milestones or by using a formal screening instrument. A resource network of more specialized medical, psychological, and educational diagnosticians can be used for follow-up and more complete assessment. Children who show signs of developmental delay or abnormal patterns of development should be immediately referred for a more comprehensive evaluation.

Case Management, Resource Linkage, and Interagency Coordination

The purpose of case management is to direct families to those community agencies, programs, and resources that most appropriately meet their identified needs. Many families will need concurrent assistance from several service systems and professional disciplines. These might include medicine, education, supplemental income, developmental programs, mental health, and social services. However, these services are generally offered through an array of programs that are not usually organized into a cooperative network. Most families find "service shopping" a tedious and often fruitless process.

In addition, some families may feel uncomfortable working with formal social service agencies. The identification and development of community-based and culturally appropriate services is helpful in assuring that families will utilize needed resources and will continue to be involved with them after the child welfare agency case is closed.

Case management and case planning form the foundation of social service delivery in any setting. Complex family needs make case assessment and planning the essential first step in any service intervention for a child with a disability. Case management should be carried out by professionals who can oversee assessment of the child's and family's needs, set goals with the family, and manage the development of a clearly defined intervention plan. Workers must also follow up to determine the effectiveness of services. Case management professionals must be thoroughly familiar with community resources if they are to guide families to appropriate services in a timely and consistent manner.

In addition to the usual range of family support resources, child welfare agencies must be linked to special programs and services for children with developmental disabilities and should develop formal interagency agreements with these service providers. This will facilitate referral, case coordination, and collaborative case planning. Coordination by service agencies, with the family as a central member of this planning team, can greatly increase the effectiveness and efficiency of all services.

Respite Care

In a recent survey of biological, foster, and adoptive parents of children with developmental disabilities, respite care was one of the most frequently cited service needs [Petr & Barney 1993]. Respite care should be viewed primarily as a form of support. Locating competent persons to care for a child with exceptional needs is a major problem for many parents. Simple activities, such as grocery shopping or going to a movie, may not be possible for a family when appropriate child care is not available. Parental employment outside the home is often impossible.

Typical child welfare services such as homemaker, day care, parent aide, protective day care, emergency shelter care, and regular foster home care could be utilized to offer short-term respite services. Homemakers with special training could provide in-home child care while parents run errands or attend to other family responsibilities. Placement of the child in a day care or day foster home might enable a parent to work outside the home. These resources can also provide short-term child care. In situations of potential child abuse, protective day care can be incorporated into the case plan. Regular foster homes may also be used to care for children on a 24-hour basis for short periods.

Child welfare agencies currently operate substitute care systems that can be modified or expanded to care for children with disabilities who need placement. Families who have had experience in caring for children with disabilities could be recruited, licensed, and trained as day care or foster care providers. Many families in the community might be willing to provide substitute care for brief periods, rather than accepting placement responsibility for a child for weeks or months. Financing such homes might be supplemented by the usual babysitting fees paid by the family. The equipment needed for care of a child with special needs can often be provided by the child's family for the duration of the respite period.

Trained foster families can also be used as mentors to educate, train, and support parents in providing proper care for their children. Parents can learn skills to provide care to their child in the foster home, under the direction and supervision of specially trained foster caregivers. The direct involvement in caregiving can help to maintain the parent-child relationship while assuring that the child's special needs are met. Foster families can also provide intermittent respite care for the family after the child returns home.

Respite services are not available in some communities and are limited in others. A comprehensive community network of respite services would be a valuable service addition in most communities, particularly if such a network could be funded, organized, and managed collaboratively by the child welfare agency, the local mental retardation/developmental disabilities service system, and the local children's mental health system.

Specialized Foster or Kinship Care Placement

Some children with developmental disabilities need longer-term placement in substitute care. Assessing the child's need for substitute care and planning for permanence does not differ from such planning for any child. Issues relating to separation trauma, visiting, and adjustment reactions to placement are universal. Foster caregivers for children with developmental disabilities must also have the skills and resources to meet the child's special needs. They may have to be specially recruited and trained. The home study for these families should be similar to that carried out for older-child adoption, with particular attention given to the family's prior experiences with disabilities and the availability of external support systems. Families may have to be trained in medical management, special aspects of daily care, behavior management, and location of community services and resources. Foster or kinship care families will also need the continuing support of the agency and other foster caregivers to manage and plan for the child.

Adoption

Child welfare's emphasis on permanence for children with special needs has increased the numbers of children with disabilities available for adoption. Yet, systemic barriers to the successful adoption of these children remain. Misconceptions held by many child welfare workers and managers have been identified as one of these significant barriers. Coyne and Brown [1985] noted that:

> Developmentally disabled children are usually perceived as especially hard to place for adoption. This perception appears to be based on informal discussions among workers and on the assumption that seriously handicapped children are extremely hard to parent and thus less desirable to potential adoptive parents. Also, their adoptive placements are thought to be more likely to disrupt than those of other children

Wimmer and Richardson [1990] identify similar barriers:

> Children [with disabilities] who were legally free for adoption were often not brought to the attention of potential adoptive families. Many children were not listed on exchanges or in photolisting books because child welfare workers, supervisors, and agency directors considered the children unadoptable. Social workers often feel that they would not wish to parent a particular child and question the motives of interested adoptive families. Eighteen percent of ... foster children [with disabilities] had as their goal "permanent foster care" and 17% had "continued foster care" rather than goals that provided permanence.

Coyne and Brown [1985] collected data that contradict these assumptions. In a survey of 799 agencies in 49 states, eight provinces, and the District of Columbia, during a 12-month period, 1,588 children with developmental disabilities had been placed for adoption. The following characteristics were identified:

- Of those 1,588, 44.5% were of school age and 9.5% were age 13 or over when they were adopted.

- Only 26% were adopted by foster parents; at least 70% were adopted by other families.

- The majority of the children placed were mentally retarded or had cerebral palsy. Placement workers had identified 31% of the children as having mild impairments, 38% with moderate impairments, 18% with severe impairments, and 5% with profound impairments.

- Boys and girls were adopted about equally. Of the children, 66% were white, 14% black, 5% Hispanic, 4% Asian, and 2% Native American.

- More than half (53%) of the adoptions were supported by an adoption subsidy.

The authors also reported an overall placement disruption rate of 8.7%. Disruption was only 3.3% when the children were 7 years of age and younger when adopted; the disruption rate for children 8 and over was 17.7%. The general disruption rate for foster parent adoptions was 4.4%, and for adoptions by a new family, 10.4%. The authors concluded that a large number of children of all ages and disabilities had been successfully placed for adoption, with a low rate of disruption.

Many child welfare agencies have modified existing adoption programs or have developed special adoption programs for children with disabilities. There are several factors in adoption programming that increase the likelihood of successful placement of children with disabilities:

- *Recruitment and education.* Potential adoptive families have to be recruited and trained regarding the special needs of children with disabilities and the special responsibilities of the families who adopt them. Targeted recruitment can help identify parents who have already reared children with disabilities. In addition, relatives and foster caregivers should routinely be considered as prospective adoptive families for the children in their care who cannot be returned home.

- *Adoption subsidy.* The availability of subsidy money may determine whether a family can adopt a child with a disability. The adoption can be supported by providing the family with the necessary financial resources to fund medical and other special services.

- *Home study.* The home study process will not differ significantly from any well-formulated home study for older children or other children with special needs. It should prepare a family for adoption, as well as assess their interests, capabilities, and limitations. Discussion regarding the special aspects of an individual child's care should be regularly included in the study.

- *Postplacement supportive services.* Most families will need considerable postplacement follow-up. Support groups that include other adoptive, foster, and biological parents of children with disabilities can offer families a helpful support system and resource network. The groups also can be educational or therapeutic in nature. Adoptive families should also be linked to the proper community services.

- *Developmental services.* Developmental services include activities that promote development and provide compensatory strategies to help assure optimum growth. Developmental services should include a program of parent education in the skills and attitudes necessary for the care and management of children with disabilities. (Parent education groups often provide a support network for the participants as well.) Topics of frequent interest include the following:

  - Behavior management strategies;

  - Leisure time activities;

  - Time and home management;

  - How to access and use supportive community resources;

  - Issues of sexuality for persons with disabilities;

  - Providing for the needs of other children in the family;

  - Estate planning, wills, and trusts;

  - Coping with negative community attitudes and prejudices; and

  - Activities to enhance a child's growth.

Programs that offer recreational and social opportunities appropriate for children with disabilities should be accessed. Many agencies operate children's therapy or activity groups. Inclusion of children with disabilities, where possible, into these peer groups can promote healthy social interaction and a beneficial growth experience for all participants.

Infant stimulation programs can train parents to provide developmental interventions. Regular participation can enhance normal development and minimize developmental delay. Preschool programs can address the developmental needs of many children with disabilities within the integrated preschool environment. Supplemental educational and recreational activities for children can also be provided.

Special Education

In 1975, Congress passed P. L. 94-142, The Education for Handicapped Children Act. Prior to this time, public schools were not required to provide educational programming for all children with disabilities. P.L. 94–142 required that school districts provide a "free, appropriate, public education" for all children with disabilities in the least restrictive environment. Individual Education Plans (IEPs) were also required, based on a complete assessment of the child's educational and developmental needs.

Since 1975, there has been considerable evidence of the benefits of early identification of children with disabilities and of early intervention. In 1986, P.L.99–457 was passed, amending P.L. 94-142 to include children between the ages of 3 and 5. The law set forth provisions to identify and provide intervention for infants and toddlers as well. These amendments are now known as the Individuals with Disabilities Education Act (IDEA) of 1991.

These laws set forth different service requirements for children at different ages. The infants and toddlers age group includes children who have diagnosed disabilities, as well as children who are at established risk because of a diagnosed medical, physical, or mental condition that has a high probability of resulting in developmental delay. Individual Family Service Plans (IFSPs) provide early intervention services to eligible children and their families. These plans are written with parental involvement and consent and generally involve a variety of community agencies in providing these services. Every local jurisdiction has an interagency collaborative group that coordinates early intervention services.

Children age 3 to 5 who have an identified disability are eligible for preschool services. Parents and educators jointly develop an IEP for these children, based on an assessment of the child's developmental needs. Public schools are responsible for providing preschool programming for these children in the least restrictive environment.

School-age children with disabilities also have an IEP developed annually. This plan guides individualized and group instruction, in the least restrictive environment, to meet the educational and developmental goals for the children.

The IFSP and IEP processes are based upon several underlying premises:

- Families are considered essential contributors in planning services for their children and have the right and ability to make decisions about their children. These include, but are not restricted to, choices of services, location of services, and the providers of the services.

- Parents also retain the right to review and receive copies of their children's records, the right to participate in meetings about their children, and the right to request testing for the child by an interdisciplinary team.

- Parents can also request that someone else represent them at a meeting with school personnel. If parents cannot attend, a guardian for the child, or educational surrogate, can attend in place of the parent.

- If a parent disagrees with findings in an evaluation or a decision made about the child's education, a due process hearing can be requested, at which time the parent's concerns will be heard and considered.

- Parents have specific responsibilities related to educational and service planning for their children. They should be prepared to participate in the IFSP or IEP process, should participate with school personnel and other professionals in a collaborative manner, and should contribute information to assist in developing the most appropriate plan for the child.

Many parents will need assistance in negotiating the school environment and in advocating for their child's developmental and educational needs. Petr and Barney [1993] contend that interventions to provide special education are a vital but underemphasized component of efforts to maintain children with disabilities in their families, and Barth [1988] found that special education problems were a critical variable in adoption disruptions. Advocating for children in the educational environment is an essential child welfare intervention.

The IFSP is, in many ways, similar to a child welfare case plan. Both address developmental goals for the child, both provide in-home and supportive services to families, and both utilize a variety of community service providers. The child welfare case plan includes an additional component, when necessary, to assure safety and protection for the child. When child welfare agencies serve children from birth to 3, with or at risk of disabilities, the family assessment and case planning process should be conducted collaboratively with personnel responsible for the IFSP. Otherwise, there is a strong possibility of duplication of effort and confusion for the family.

Counseling and Emotional Support

Most families of children with disabilities will, at some time, need significant emotional support. The birth of a child with a disability can promote crisis in some families. Depression and anxiety are common. Considerable stress may be placed on the marital relationship, and siblings may develop behavior or emotional problems. In addition, children and youth with disabilities may also exhibit depression or anxiety, which contributes to behavior disorders. This may often remain unidentified by caregivers and by some mental health practitioners.

Families of children with disabilities report several sources of emotional support. These include extended family, intimate friends, church contacts, neighbors, community groups, clubs, work place acquaintances, and human services professionals [Wikler 1986]. However, Petr and Barney's [1993] study sample indicated that parents could not always depend upon these resources for the consistent, reliable, and empathic support they needed:

> The most reliable and inspirational source of support was other parents of children with similar disabilities. These parents share a common bond that allows for understanding and support at the deepest levels. These relationships can enrich the total experience by helping parents see the positive aspects of raising a child with special needs, and by helping them appreciate their own personal growth... [Petr & Barney 1993].

This has significant implications for child welfare practice, particularly considering the previously mentioned finding that families of mentally retarded children are often socially isolated [Wikler 1986]. Agencies should make extensive use of parent groups that include biological, foster, and adoptive parents of children with disabilities. Such groups can serve multiple functions, including education and training, recreation and leisure, counseling, and peer support. It is important that group affiliations be continued even after the child welfare agency is no longer involved. For this reason, groups should be sponsored and supported by agencies that serve children with disabilities, local community agencies, advocacy groups, and the parents themselves.

The caseworker should also be alert to the need for formal mental health counseling and should help the family access the most appropriate service provider. The worker should be able to recognize families near or in crisis, the presence of acute or chronic depression or anxiety, marital and family conflict, and other signs that the family is experiencing severe stress. Counseling resources can include professional counselors, members of the clergy, local mental health agencies, counselors through mental retardation and developmental disability agencies, and culturally specific community providers.

Advocacy

Advocacy is action on behalf of, or in the interest of others. There are probably as many different types of advocacy as there are arenas wherein people need help. Advocacy can assist in accessing services, in assuring maintenance of individual rights, or in negotiating complicated systems. The need for advocacy can reflect a person's inability to independently negotiate a system, as is true for persons with developmental disabilities, or it may reflect the general complexity of the system that may overtax the capability of most in the general population.

Some systems of advocacy are an institutionalized part of our society, such as the child welfare systems, the courts, and policing agencies. Others are of grass-roots or citizen origin. Both may become legislated entities. There are several types of advocacy:

- *Legal advocacy*, generally performed by attorneys, is an effort to ensure that the legal rights and entitlements of an individual or group of individuals are not denied.

- *Systems advocacy* promotes the common rights of a particular population by negotiating and altering a designated system. Examples are advocating for better conditions in a residential institution or for the installation of ramp-style curbs on city streets.

- *Citizen or volunteer advocacy* is carried out by individual community members who assist a person in day-to-day activities and in negotiating service systems. Activities might include assisting a person with budgeting, obtaining adequate housing, filling out an application form, or locating a lost assistance check.

- *Case management advocacy* is generally performed by professionals with case management responsibility for a family. These professionals ensure that the family's needs are fully assessed, they draw up and implement a comprehensive case plan, and they locate and access the most appropriate service providers. Case management advocacy may require monitoring the services provided by other agencies and intervening to assure that such agencies deliver what they have agreed to deliver.

Advocacy activities specifically for children with disabilities and their families should address the following objectives:

- Protecting an individual or group of individuals from abuse, neglect, or exploitation. This may include identifying when decisions to withhold or terminate care for infants with life-threatening medical conditions constitute abuse or neglect.

- Promoting equal access to services and resources, such as education, employment, housing, social services, and health care resources, and assuring that resource providers make "reasonable accommodations" to enable participation of persons with disabilities.

- Promoting awareness of the rights and entitlements of a person or group and ensuring such rights. This includes educating people about their rights and assuring that service providers fully understand and implement their responsibilities under the law to provide specialized services.

- Ensuring physical accessibility to community buildings or services. This includes construction of ramps and wheelchair-accessible doorways and accessible restrooms.

- Ensuring that certain persons or groups are afforded a representative voice in decision making and legislation, particularly as it affects them.

The child welfare worker has many advocacy responsibilities. Protective service is an institutionalized form of advocacy designed to protect children from abuse, neglect, or exploitation. Part of a social worker's responsibility includes aggressively assisting the client in gaining access to and negotiating social service systems. Activities performed by child welfare workers when advocating for children with disabilities might include the following:

- Attendance at educational planning conferences with school personnel and parents to make sure that an IEP or IFSP is developed for the child and family and to assure that the child is not placed in a more restrictive, segregated educational environment than is necessary to meet the child's needs. This may also mean helping parents pursue due process when they are dissatisfied with a school's plan for their child.

- Supporting parents in their efforts to obtain appropriate services, including evaluating and identifying the best provider or resource, initiating referrals, expediting the application process, attending planning sessions, and helping parents overcome obstacles caused by negative stereotypic attitudes and restrictive policies.

- Using professional influence to deal with systems to assure that the rights of children and their families are not violated, linking with formal advocacy agencies, and obtaining legal representation, when necessary.

- Assuring that the child's best interests are reflected in the agency's case plan for that child.

- Advocating for expedient and effective interagency coordination on behalf of the family. The child welfare caseworker, as a case management advocate, will often intervene to provide direction to other service providers to assure service coordination. Parent aides, volunteers, and foster caregivers can also be trained to serve in a case management and coordination role, once the case plan has been developed.

Parent-Professional Relationships

Families in Petr and Barney's [1993] study had strong opinions about the qualities of professionals they found to be helpful—and not helpful. Most often, criticism of professionals was related to the perception that many professionals believed the children would be "better off in placement," despite parents' wishes to keep their children at home. While parents understood this to be based on well-intentioned concern for meeting the child's therapeutic or educational needs, it was perceived as intrusive and unwarranted. Parents communicated their desire that their children be integrated as much as possible into the "mainstream" of community life, so their children's lives could be as normal as possible. They wanted professionals to help them do so. This required avoiding labels and preconceived ideas about the child's disability—in other words, "see the child and not the disability."

Families also listed the qualities and behaviors they found helpful in their caseworkers. They appreciated such worker activities as the following:

- Spending more time to get to know the child and family, to understand their issues, and to become a part of their support network before offering solutions or advice and relating to parents as peers and collaborators rather than as "distant experts";

- Demonstrating an ability to listen and show respect for the parents' opinions and feelings and allowing the parents to disagree and have a different view without jeopardizing the relationship;

- Not being inappropriately pessimistic about the child's potential; expressing realistic optimism about the child's successes and gains;

- Avoiding negative stereotypes and misconceptions and helping families promote normalization and community integration for their children;

- Providing families with essential information to help them access special services or programs;

- Avoiding unwarranted criticism or blame about what was wrong in the family or what the parents had done wrong; and

- Helping the family access services that could prevent the exacerbation of stress and crisis that could lead to placement.

Case Example

Elena was injured by her 19-year-old uncle, Tony, when she was 7 months old. Tony was babysitting while Elena's mother, Diane, went grocery shopping. After Elena had cried nonstop for several hours, Tony picked Elena up and shook her. When Diane came home, she could not wake Elena. She became frightened and took the baby to the emergency room. Elena had suffered a severe subdural hematoma, or blood clot in the brain, as a result of having been shaken. The hospital called the child welfare agency and referred Elena for suspected abuse. The case was opened and transferred to a family services caseworker.

The worker learned that Diane and Tony were relatively new to the city, having moved there from a small town to find work after their mother had died. They had no other family and few friends in the area. Their only relatives were distant cousins in another state. The whereabouts of Elena's father were not known.

Elena remained in the hospital. Diane visited her daily. As the days passed, the seriousness of Elena's injuries became evident. She developed seizures. She was initially severely hypotonic, with a serious lack of muscle tone, but then developed increasing spasticity. She was eventually diagnosed with epilepsy and cerebral palsy, both believed to be the result of a serious head injury from shaking. It was too early to determine whether she would be mentally retarded.

Diane was devastated. She reacted by angrily attacking the doctors and demanding additional opinions. She threatened a lawsuit against the hospital. She then went into clinical crisis. She was alternately angry and profoundly depressed. She threatened to kill her brother and then swore she would kill herself. The child welfare worker immediately called the crisis center at the mental health agency and transported Diane to the first appointment. The crisis counselor saw Diane every day for a week and three times weekly, afterward. The child welfare worker continued to contact Diane regularly, and confer with the crisis counselor. The crisis counselor helped Diane begin to deal with her situation. Diane said she was strongly considering placing Elena for adoption, since she did not believe herself capable of caring for a child with a serious disability.

The crisis worker and the child welfare worker met jointly with Diane to map out a plan that would help her eventually make a realistic decision about her ability to care for Elena. Activities included attending a support group of parents whose children had disabilities, which was run by the early intervention center in the local mental retardation/developmental disabilities agency. Diane then visited a classroom where early intervention and infant stimulation activities were being conducted. She talked with parents whose children were severely disabled and with parents whose children were making significant developmental strides in spite of their disabilities. Throughout this period, the crisis worker helped Diane begin to come to terms with the injury to her child. The crisis worker reported Diane to be angry and deeply depressed.

The child welfare worker, concerned about Tony, asked Diane's permission to contact him. The worker explained that most people did not understand that shaking a child was dangerous and wondered whether Diane thought her brother had intentionally harmed Elena. Diane didn't think so, but thought him immature and seriously lacking in judgment. She was still too furious at him to even talk to him and didn't know whether she ever could.

The child welfare worker called and set an appointment to talk with Tony. He agreed to meet with her only after considerable prodding and the reassurance that his involvement would ultimately be important to Elena and Diane. The worker also communicated she was greatly concerned about him. When they finally met, Tony was extremely upset. He told the worker he felt totally responsible for the "accident." He cried throughout the interview. He reported being unable to go to work. He looked like he hadn't slept for weeks. With encouragement, Tony allowed the worker to schedule an appointment with the crisis counselor that afternoon. The worker transported him. The crisis counselor continued to see Tony for several weeks and was eventually able to do joint counseling with Diane and Tony.

After several weeks, Elena was discharged to the rehabilitation unit of Children's Hospital, where she was to stay while she received physical therapy and ongoing medical intervention. The worker suggested that Diane stay with Elena during the week and participate in the rehabilitation activities. Diane refused. She felt if she were going to place Elena for adoption, she should do so and not prolong the inevitable. However, she said she wasn't ready to sign any papers just yet and asked to be left alone.

The child welfare worker arranged a joint meeting with Diane and the crisis worker to discuss Diane's concerns. During this session, Diane was helped to understand that her desire to place Elena resulted from terror that she would hurt Elena and her despair that, if she retained custody of Elena, she would never have a life for herself. Yet she could not bring herself to give up her child. The crisis worker assured Diane that her ambivalence was normal and that it was probably premature to make a final decision. The child welfare worker suggested a three-month trial period, wherein Diane could be taught to care for Elena, and the worker would help her plan her own life as well. At the end of three months, they would again evaluate Diane's feelings. The worker made it clear that whichever course Diane chose, adoption or keeping Elena, the worker would help her develop the best permanent plan possible for Elena.

The child welfare worker contacted hospital social services and arranged for Diane to stay in a boarding home near the hospital. The agency paid the nominal cost for room and board. Tony offered to transport her each week so she could stay with Elena and to transport her home on the weekend. Diane grudgingly agreed.

The hospital social worker involved Diane in the activities of the rehabilitation center. The physical therapist taught her how to exercise and stimulate Elena without hurting her. The psychologist talked to Diane about the importance of stimulation and affection and helped her be less afraid of handling Elena. Under the guidance of the psychologist, Diane began taking over more responsibility for parenting Elena at the hospital. At first, Diane was upset because Elena didn't seem to recognize or respond to her. With ongoing support from the psychologist, she continued to cuddle, hold, and talk to Elena, and eventually, Elena began to respond to her by smiling and cooing. This was quite reinforcing for Diane.

When Elena was ready for discharge a month later, Diane was still too afraid to have sole responsibility for her. She wanted the baby to remain in the rehabilitation unit, and when told this was not possible, she resumed talk about placing Elena for adoption. The child welfare worker provided Diane with a third alternative. She located a woman, Eloise Watkins, through the mental retardation/developmental disabilities early intervention center. Ms. Watkins had raised her own child (who had cerebral palsy) and now did volunteer work at the center. She agreed to care for Elena on a temporary basis and to work with Diane. The child welfare worker arranged for Diane and herself to visit the Watkins home. After meeting Eloise, seeing her home, and meeting her 21-year-old daughter, Diane agreed to the placement.

The worker arranged for Diane to visit Elena in the foster home each day. Under the guidance of the foster mother, Diane took on more and more responsibility for Elena's direct care. At Eloise's prodding, she sometimes brought Tony with her. He had returned to work, but consistently expressed a desire to learn how to care for Elena so he could help Diane. Diane was initially reluctant, said emphatically she would never leave Elena home alone with him again, but eventually agreed to have him along.

Diane also accompanied Elena and Eloise to the early intervention center, where she participated in infant stimulation. Eventually Diane picked up Elena at the foster home and took her to the center independently. As Diane gained confidence in caring for Elena, she agreed to a trial period with Elena at home. The foster mother and child welfare worker helped Diane acquire the necessary equipment she would need at home. Elena began going home for weekends. Finally, at age 14 months, Elena went home under Diane's care.

Diane received ongoing services and support from the early intervention center and from the child welfare agency. She often became overwhelmed, but her brother insisted she become involved—and stay involved—in the parent support group. He also attended these groups, and he utilized the group support to deal with his own guilt and emotional pain. Diane kept in contact with the crisis worker and on occasion went in for counseling sessions. The child welfare worker provided continued case management and advocacy to assure that Diane was linked to all the necessary medical and support services. She also helped Diane apply for financial subsidies.

Elena was enrolled in the county infant stimulation program under IDEA, where she could receive ongoing services. At the end of the three-month trial period, Diane agreed to parent Elena permanently but expressed considerable fear about being left without support. The child welfare worker made certain that Diane remained linked to community support services before she closed the case. She called Diane periodically to see how she was doing.

Epilogue

Elena's seizures were eventually controlled by anticonvulsant medication. As Elena continued to develop her motor skills, she eventually learned to sit and stand with assistance. Her diagnosis was changed to cerebral palsy of moderate involvement, and it was thought that with continued physical therapy, Elena might be able to walk with braces. Early indications were that Elena would likely be within the normal range of intelligence. She was alert, interested in her surroundings, and appeared to understand words at about 18 months. Tony visited often, played with Elena, helped with her physical therapy, and brought her toys and books. Diane often called him to watch Elena to enable her to work around the house, read a book, or relax; however, she refused to let him stay alone with Elena and continued to take Elena to the Watkins home for respite and babysitting. Diane continued to be involved with parent support groups, and other community services. She eventually began to talk about returning to school to train for a career.

REFERENCES

Abroms, I. F. (1980a). The child with a seizure disorder. In A. P. Scheiner & I. F. Abroms (Eds.), *The practical management of the developmentally disabled child*. St. Louis: C.V. Mosby Co.

Abroms, I. F. (1980b). The child with significant developmental motor disability (Cerebral palsy: Medical and neurological aspects). In A. P. Scheiner & I. F. Abroms (Eds.), *The practical management of the developmentally disabled child*. St. Louis: C.V. Mosby Co.

American Association of Mental Retardation. (1992). *AAMR diagnosis, classification, and systems of supports*. Washington, DC: Author.

American Psychiatric Association. (1994). *Diagnostic and statistical manual of mental disorders (DSM-IV)* (4th ed.). Washington, DC: Author.

Anday, E. K., Cohen, M. E., Kelley, N. E., & Leitner, D. S. (1989). Effect of in-utero cocaine exposure on startle and its modification. *Dev Pharmacol Ther*, 12(3), 137-145.

Azuma, S. D., & Chasnoff, I. J. (1993). Outcome of children prenatally exposed to cocaine and other drugs: A path analysis of three-year data. *Pediatrics*, 92(3), 396-402.

Barth, R. P. (1988). Disruption in older child adoptions. *Public Welfare*, 46, p. 23-29. As cited in Petr, C. G. & Barney, D. D. (1993). Reasonable efforts for children with disabilities: The parents' perspective. *Social Work*, 38(3), 247-254.

Bartoshesky, L.E. (1980). Genetics and the child with developmental disabilities. In A. P. Scheiner & I. F. Abroms (Eds.), *The practical management of the developmentally disabled child*. St. Louis: C.V. Mosby Co.

Beckman, P. J. (1983). Influence of selected child characteristics on stress in families of handicapped infants. *American Journal of Mental Deficiency, 88*(2), 150-156.

Besharov, D. J. (Ed.). (1994) *When drug addicts have children*. Washington, DC: Child Welfare League of America.

Caruso, K. & ten Bensel, R. (1993). Fetal alcohol syndrome and fetal alcohol effects. *Minnesota Medicine, 76*, 25-29.

Chase, H. P., & Martin, H. P. (1970). Undernutrition and child development. *New England Journal of Medicine, 282*, 933-939.

Chasnoff, I. J., Griffith, D. R., MacGregor, S., Dirkes, K., & Burns, K. A. (1989a). Temporal patterns of cocaine use in pregnancy: Perinatal outcome. *Journal of the American Medical Association, 261*(12), 1741-1744.

Chasnoff, I. J., Hunt, C. E., Kletter, R., & Kaplan, D. (1989b). Prenatal cocaine exposure is associated with respiratory pattern abnormalities. *American Journal Disabled Children 143*(5), 583-7.

Chasnoff, I. J., Lewis, D. E., Griffith, D. R., & Willey, S. (1989c). Cocaine and pregnancy: Clinical and toxicological implications for the neonate. *Clinical Chemistry 35*(7), 1276-8.

Chavkin, W., Paone, D., Friedmann, P., & Wilets, I. (1993). Reframing the debate: Toward effective treatment for inner city drug-abusing mothers. *Bulletin of the New York Academy of Medicine, 70*(1).

Cherukuri, R., Minkoff, H., Feldman, J., Parekh, A., & Glass, L. (1988). A cohort study of alkaloidal cocaine ("crack") in pregnancy. *Obstetrics and Gynecology, 72*(2), 147-51.

Coyne, A., & Brown, M. E. (1985). Developmentally disabled children can be adopted. *Child Welfare, 64*(6), 607-616.

Coyne, A., & Brown, M. E. (1986). Relationship between foster care and adoption units serving developmentally disabled children. *Child Welfare, 65*(2), 189-198.

Doberczak, T. M., Shanzer, S., Senie, R. T., & Kandall, S. R. (1988). Neonatal neurologic and electroencephalographic effects of intrauterine cocaine exposure. *Journal of Pediatrics, 113*(2), 354-8.

Dyson, L. (1991). Families of young children with handicaps: Parental stress and family functioning. *American Journal on Mental Retardation,* *95*(6), 623-629.

Falconer, J. (1982). Health care delivery problems for the disabled. In M. G. Eisenberg, C. Griggins, & R. J . Duval (Eds.), *Disabled people as second class citizens.* New York: Springer.

Fulroth, R., Phillips, B., & Durand, D. J. (1989). Perinatal outcome of infants exposed to cocaine and/or heroin in utero. *Am J. Dis Child, 143*(8), 905-910.

Griffith, D. R., Azuma, S. D., & Chasnoff, I. J. (1994). Three-year outcome of children exposed prenatally to drugs. *Journal of the American Academy of Child and Adolescent Psychiatry. 33*(l), 20-27.

Hadeed, A. J., & Siegel, S. R. (1989). Maternal cocaine use during pregnancy: Effect on the newborn infant. *Pediatrics, 84*(2), 205-210.

Helfer, R. E., McKinney, J., & Kempe, R. (1976). Arresting or freezing the developmental process. In R. E. Helfer & C. H. Kempe, *Child abuse and neglect: The family and the community.* Cambridge, MA: Ballinger Publishing Company.

Howard, J., Beckwith, L., Rodning, C., & Kropenske, M. P. H. (1989). The development of young children of substance-abusing parents: Insights from seven years of intervention and research. *Zero to Three,* June.

Institute for Child Advocacy. (1987). *Children in out-of-home care.* Cleveland, OH: Institute for Child Advocacy.

Jones, K. L. & Smith, D. W. (1973). Recognition of the fetal alcohol syndrome in early infancy. *Lancet, ii,* 999-1001.

Kanner, L. (1973). *Childhood psychosis: Initial studies and new insight.* Washington, DC: V. H. Winston and Sons.

Kurtz, P. D. (1979). Early identification of handicapped children: A time for social work involvement. *Child Welfare, 58*(3), 165-176.

Levine, M. D. (1980). The child with learning disabilities. In A. P. Scheiner & I. F. Abroms (Eds.), *The practical management of the developmentally disabled child.* St. Louis: C.V. Mosby Co.

Little, B. B., Snell, L. M., Klein, V. R., & Gilstrap, L. C. (1989). Cocaine abuse during pregnancy: Maternal and fetal implications. *Obstetrics and Gynecology, 73*(2), February, 157-60.

MacGregor, S. N., Keith, L. G., Chasnoff, I. J., Rosner, M. A., Chisum, G. M., Shaw, P., & Minogue, J. P. (1987). Cocaine use during pregnancy: Adverse perinatal outcomes. *Am J. Obstet Gynecol, 157*(3), 686-69.

Martin, H. (1972). The child and his development. In C. H. Kempe & R. E. Helfer, (Eds.), *Helping the battered child and his family*. Philadelphia: Lippincott, 93-114.

Martin, J. E. & Laidlow, T. T. (1980). Implications of direct service planning, delivery and policy. In A. R. Novak & L. W. Heal, (Eds.), *Integration of developmentally disabled individuals into the community*. Baltimore: Paul H. Brooks.

McCubbin, H. & Patterson, J. (1983). Family stress adaptation to crises: A double ABCX model of family behavior. In H. McCubbin, M. Sussman, & J. Patterson (Eds.), *Social stresses and the family: Advances and developments in family stress theory and research*. New York: The Haworth Press. As cited in Wikler, L. M. (1986). Family stress theory and research on families of children with mental retardation. In J. J. Gallagher & P. M. Vietze (Eds.), *Families of handicapped persons: Research, programs, and policy issues* (pp. 167-195). Baltimore: Paul Brookes.

National Research Council, Panel on Research on Child Abuse and Neglect, Commission on Behavioral and Social Sciences and Education (1993). *Understanding child abuse and neglect*. Washington, DC: National Academy Press.

Ornitz, E. M., & Ritvo, E. R . (1976). The syndrome of autism: A critical review. *American Journal of Psychiatry, 133*(6).

Parad, H. J., & Caplan, G. (1965). A framework for studying families in crisis. In H. Parad & G. Caplan (Eds.), *Crisis intervention: Selected readings*. New York: Family Service Association of America.

Petr, C. G. & Barney, D. D. (1993). Reasonable efforts for children with disabilities: The parents' perspective. *Social Work, 38*(3), 247-254.

Rapoport, L. (1965). The state of crisis: Some theoretical considerations. In H. Parad & G. Caplan (Eds.), *Crisis intervention: Selected readings*. New York: Family Service Association of America.

Richardson, M., West, M. A., Day, P., & Stuart, S. (1989). Children with developmental disabilities in the child welfare system: A national survey. *Child Welfare, 68*(6), 605-614.

Ross Laboratories. (1989). *Cocaine babies. Special currents.* Columbus, Ohio: Ross Laboratories.

Scherling, D. (1994). Prenatal cocaine exposure and childhood psychopathology: A developmental analysis. *American Journal of Orthopsychiatry, 64*(1), 9-19.

Schilling, R. F., Kirkham, M. A., & Schinke, S. P. (1986). Do child protection services neglect developmentally disabled children? *Education and Training of the Mentally Retarded, 21*(1), 21-26.

Smith, D. W. (1982). *Recognizable patterns of human malformation: Genetic and embryologic and clinical aspects* (3rd ed.). Philadelphia: W.B. Saunders Co.

Spohr, H. L., Willms, J., & Steinhausen, H. C. (1993). Prenatal alcohol exposure and long-term developmental consequences. *The Lancet, 341,* 907-11.

Steele, B. (1987). Psychodynamic factors in child abuse. In R. E. Helfer & R. S. Kempe (Eds.), *The battered child* (4th ed.). Chicago: University of Chicago Press.

Steinhausen, H. C., Willms, J., & Spohr, H. L. (1993). Long-term psychopathological and cognitive outcomes of children with fetal alcohol syndrome. *Journal of the American Academy of Child and Adolescent Psychiatry, 32*(5), 990-994.

Thain, W. S., Casto, G., & Peterson, A. (1980). *Normal and handicapped children: A growth and development primer for parents and professionals.* Littleton, MA: PSG Publishing Co., Inc.

Wikler, L. M. (1986). Family stress theory and research on families of children with mental retardation. In J. J. Gallagher & P. M. Vietze (Eds.), *Families of handicapped persons: Research, programs, and policy issues* (167-195). Baltimore: Paul Brookes.

Wimmer, J., & Richardson, S. (1990). Adoption of children with developmental disabilities. *Child Welfare, 69*(6), 563-569.

Zuckerman, B., Frank, D. A., Hingson, R., Amaro, H., Levenson, S. M., Kayne, H., Parker, S., Vinci, R., Aboagye, K., & Fried, L. E. (1989). Effects of maternal marijuana and cocaine use on fetal growth. *New England Journal of Medicine 23*, 762-768.

ABOUT THE AUTHORS

 **Ronald C. Hughes,** Ph.D., has a diverse educational background, with degrees in philosophy and social administration, as well as a doctorate in developmental psychology, which he received from The Ohio State University in 1989. He has worked as a public human services caseworker, a drug rehabilitation counselor, clinical director of a residential treatment facility for youth, an individual and family counselor, and a child welfare administrator.

 **Judith S. Rycus,** Ph.D., launched her child welfare career as an adoption caseworker in Los Angeles County, California. She completed her M.S.W. degree at Wayne State University in 1972 and worked as a child protective services supervisor and trainer in Columbus, Ohio. She received her Ph.D. in developmental psychology in 1990, with specialization in developmental disabilities and organizational development.

Dr. Hughes and Dr. Rycus founded the **Institute for Human Services** in 1977. Over the past 20 years, they have greatly advanced the child welfare field with their books, monographs, articles, training resources, consultation, and leadership. They are the architects of the Comprehensive, Competency-Based Inservice Training (CCBIT) System for child welfare and have helped to establish and operate large-scale training systems in child welfare organizations throughout North America. They also co-authored the *Field Guide to Child Welfare*, the comprehensive resource textbook from which this monograph was reproduced.

Field Guide to Child Welfare

Judith S. Rycus & Ronald C. Hughes

CWLA Press is pleased to announce the publication of the *Field Guide to Child Welfare*, by Judith S. Rycus and Ronald C. Hughes. The Child Welfare league of America (CWLA) and the Institute for Human Services in Columbus, Ohio, collaborated to publish this comprehensive, four-volume resource for child welfare workers and supervisors to use in their everyday practice.

The 1,000+ page *Field Guide* describes basic theory, practical application, and pertinent case examples. This guide examines specialized such practice issues as adoption, sexual abuse, cultural competency, and children with developmental disabilities.

The *Field Guide* was designed to be thorough, pragmatic, and well grounded in principle. A required resource for anyone who works in child welfare and related fields.